Peeling The Layers

Gary Larson

outskirts
press

Peeling Back The Layers
All Rights Reserved.
Copyright © 2021 Gary Larson
v2.0

This is a work of fiction. Names, characters, businesses, places, events, locales, and incidents are either the products of the author's imagination or used in a fictitious manner. Any resemblance to actual persons, living or dead, or actual events is purely coincidental.

The opinions expressed in this manuscript are solely the opinions of the author and do not represent the opinions or thoughts of the publisher. The author has represented and warranted full ownership and/or legal right to publish all the materials in this book.

This book may not be reproduced, transmitted, or stored in whole or in part by any means, including graphic, electronic, or mechanical without the express written consent of the publisher except in the case of brief quotations embodied in critical articles and reviews.

Outskirts Press, Inc.
http://www.outskirtspress.com

ISBN: 978-1-9772-3326-4

Cover Photo © 2021 Gary Larson. All rights reserved - used with permission.

Outskirts Press and the "OP" logo are trademarks belonging to Outskirts Press, Inc.

PRINTED IN THE UNITED STATES OF AMERICA

No one can tell a good yarn like an old sea dog, and Gary Larson is among the best. As a sailor and a pastor, his stories are balm for the heart and sugar for the soul. His collection of tales reveals a life well-lived – with all the bumps and bruises, victories and defeats revealed. Anyone who has spun the wheel of a sailing ship, marveled at the miracle of a spider's web, or loved another person will recognize themselves in these heart-warming sagas from a man in love with life.

Brian Pitzer, friend,
publicist, and writer

Gary Larson's essays are at times humorous, at times nostalgic, at times curmudgeonly, but they are always thoughtful and reflective.

Marlene Lang, friend, adjunct
instructor of composition

It's impossible for me to read this book without hearing these stories and reflections delivered in Gary's deep, rumbling voice. He really is in these pages. Pastor, sailor, and a thousand other things, Gary has raised being a backyard philosopher to an art form, which is no small feat. I loved the book. It's all over the place in the best possible way!

Allan Carpenter, friend,
radio DJ and news anchor

A little humor. A little sermon by the sea. Start anywhere and hope you have a friend on speed dial. You're gonna wanna share. A classic Larson ramble. He has opinions on God, taxes, Moby-Dick, and Mum the Ghostbuster. The man was born to preach.

Linda Ague, friend,
middle school librarian

CONTENTS

INTRODUCTION i
1. ROGUE WAVES... 1
2. FOREVER HOPEFUL...3
3. SETTLER OR PIONEER...6
4. HIGH ON WHAT IS.. 8
5. PORCUPINES 13
6. TREES 16
7. FLOATING FREE 22
8. PROVERBS 24
9. HEY, BLACKIE 29
10. THE IN-BETWEEN…OR NOT? 33
11. AUTHORITY 34
12. OLD-TIMER BENEFITS......................................37
13. DEEP CALLS TO DEEP 44
14. THE THIN LINE BETWEEN A KICK AND A HUG 46
15. BEYOND THE PAIN OF DEATH 53
16. CAMP DUFFIELD 56
17. LOVE NEVER ENDS 57
18. FAMILY BATHROOM WARS 60
19. THUS SPAKE KOHELETH 63
20. MOBY-DICK 65
21. THROUGH A SON'S YOUNG EYES 69
22. EFFECTIVE COURTSHIP 70
23. SELF-AWARENESS..74
24. HISTORY, MYSTERY, AND THE PRESENT..................79
25. WORDS WE LIVE BY 82
26. DISTRACTION..94
27. GRANDMA'S BIG LIE 96
28. THE COMMON SENSE OF MODERATION 101
29. CONTROL 107

30. SCARS 110
31. KEEP THE SIMPLE, SIMPLE
    SO YOU CAN HANDLE THE COMPLICATED 113
32. GHOSTS ARE REAL 119
33. THE WEAK AND THE STRONG 121
34. CEMETERY RISINGS 125
35. CORRECTING EACH OTHER 127
36. THEM THAT SAYS MORE
    THAN OTHERS WANT TO HEAR 130
37. TEMPUS FUGIT 133
38. THE DAY CRASH DANCED 137

INTRODUCTION

One of my professors stood up in front on the first day of class and held up an onion. I thought to myself, *Where's this fella going with this one?* I especially wondered as the class had nothing to do with agriculture or anything close to it.

He began, "You've all seen onions before. You've probably eaten onions. But did you really know about the onion you saw or ate? Was it a cursory, or close encounter? In this class, we are going to peel away the layers of onions and discover what may lie beneath. Did you know that most onions have eight to thirteen layers, each layer somewhat smaller as one moves toward the center? Although all onions are alike, each one is unique. Each layer of each onion is unique as well. If we were to examine each layer more closely, we might learn about the uniqueness in our onions.

"Peeling onions is not a pleasant task for most people. If you've done it, you know that your eyes might begin to water or burn. Your nose might begin to drip, and you may sneeze. Before you get to the center of the onion, you might be a wet mess and very uncomfortable."

The professor continued with his object lesson. "In this class we are going to be engaging thoughts, ideas, concepts. In our daily routines, we accept most thoughts for what they are. For example, this is an onion. In this class, we are going to dig down, peel away the layers, and examine as we go. We might imagine what is in the layers, but we will move from imagination to discovery as we carefully engage each thought that may come our way. This experience may make our eyes burn and our noses drip. That is, we might be uncomfortable as we peel away the layers. Looking more closely at thoughts, ideas, concepts may disturb us, challenge us, change us. We will be richer for the experience. I hope we together can make it a journey that we'll look back upon and be glad we took."

This is what we will be doing in this book. Each chapter is a different subject—a unique onion, as it were. We'll peel away some layers and look more deeply into what our thoughts and feelings might be, and how, with a closer look, they may be changed with new insight and perspective.

1

ROGUE WAVES

I'VE BEEN A sailor for seventy years, mostly on sloops, which are what most sailboats are. A sloop has one mast and two sails. From my experience as a sailor, I want to tell you about a frightful encounter, whether it occurs on the salty oceans or the fresh water seas.

A "rogue wave" is an unpredictable wave, one that moves differently from other waves. Waves are created by wind. Wind usually blows from one direction toward the opposite direction as a wall of wind. This creates rows of waves. So, wind blows over the surface of the water, and waves then flow in the same direction. On most days, wind blows from one direction—for example, from the southeast toward the northwest. On most days, wind usually blows for many hours, perhaps increasing in velocity. Then gradually it may change to another direction and wind speed. A rogue wave comes along, seemingly with a mind of its own. A rogue wave flows against or sideways to the many other waves.

Additionally, a rogue wave is customarily larger, more powerful than other waves. In fact, that's why it is called rogue. In a sea of three-foot waves from the southwest, a rogue wave may come along at seven feet tall from the northwest, or from any other direction. Rogue waves are usually dangerous for sailors, as rogue waves are powerful and usually hit unexpectedly. A sailboat gliding along comfortably is suddenly attacked, it might be said, by a rogue wave that jolts the boat from its serenity.

A very alert sailor might see the wave and take appropriate action so that the impact is lessened. But in many cases, there is little warning. The rogue wave hits, the sailboat gets knocked over from its nearly vertical position to almost horizontal. A "heeled over" boat can tip by 80 to 90 degrees, which is called a knockdown. A rogue wave is a wake-up call like few others.

Rogue waves can be a simile or metaphor for life. We cruise along, just minding our own business, when, Bam! We're hit on the blind side, we like to say. Suddenly, something comes along to bolt us from one position into an entirely new position. We shake our heads and blurt out, "What happened?"

Generally speaking, people do not like their established views and opinions, their beliefs, and their foundation blocks for living upset and disturbed. Most don't like their thoughts to become unsettled, any more than having their sailboat encounter a rogue wave. In fact, many people become very protective of their thoughts and beliefs. But it can be good, being thrown out of the rocking chair of routine. It can be good filling in the ruts that are so deep that we don't have choice over which way we go. It can be good to almost tip over, but to recover with new insights, perspectives, and deeper experience.

In a similar way that rogue waves can be beneficial while sailing, we can learn from rogue waves as we journey through life. We learn to anticipate and pay attention, be more cautious and alert. Nevertheless, rogue waves continue to take us by surprise. But they can help us see things we hadn't seen before. They can help us understand things we hadn't understood before. They can help us be more aware and alert and prepared. Rogue waves can teach us, if we search for the lessons.

2

FOREVER HOPEFUL

MY FAMILY WAS "lower middle class" at best. We did have meat every night, but summer vacations were few. Everyone in my family worked: mother, father, brother, me.

Mom and Dad were not college educated. Going to college was not an option for them. But what they could not have, they surely did want for their two sons. Their sons would have a college education, no matter how hard it would be to achieve that goal. They worked for years in the hopes of that reality. After my father died when I was in 10th grade, money got even tighter. Without Dad's income and with a measly death benefit, we three pressed on with the endless task of earning money.

I peddled newspapers for years. In winter, I shoveled snow off sidewalks and driveways. During the summer months, there were various jobs. I bussed tables in restaurants. I stacked beer cases in a brewery. I mopped floors and stacked food on grocery shelves. I was a "Fuller Brush Man." I delivered furniture for a department store. I was a night watchman. I degreased and cleaned industrial equipment shelves. I repaired bicycles.

Even during college breaks I worked. During Christmas break, I would head down to Man Power, an agency that linked day laborers with companies needing temporary help. Those who showed up for Man Power were of two types: college students and drunks. If the job required two people, the agency would likely link up one of each.

So, I was assigned to Charlie Talbot. Naturally, he didn't have a car, but I did, sort of. It was a sixteen-year-old Chevy, but it got us there. Our job was to unload two railroad cars of their lumber cargo. The task would take several days due to the quantity. Also, as the shipment came from northwest Canada, most of the boards were frozen to each other.

The site foreman showed and shouted to us, "Get this job done in three days and there'll be extra money in it for both of you." Unless you have ever hand unloaded boards from a rail car, you have no idea how many boards and how much weight in wood is in one railroad car. But the lure of "extra money" caught the attention of both of us. We put our minds and bodies to it. We finished almost three-quarters of the first car on day one. Our sore muscles were the proof.

"Hey," my partner Charlie said to me, "you coming tomorrow?"

"I expect I will. I'll pick you up at Man Power at 6 a.m.," I said.

Day two was colder and snowier than the first, but the two of us pressed on. We developed a relay system which was time and energy efficient. We began sweating, even with the chilly winter temperatures. Less than ten minutes for our packed lunches, then back to work until 5 p.m. when it became too dark to see.

"I think we're going to make it," Charlie said to me at the end of day two. "I'll see you tomorrow."

Day three of hard, hard labor began with muscles so tight and sore we both could barely move. But we dove into the task motivated by the bonus pay we both expected to receive. Just before 5 p.m., we stacked the last board on the platform. The site boss showed up with the extra pay, $10 each, which was a big tip in those days. We both counted the take in our shivering hands.

Charlie looked at me and said, "You didn't do too bad for a college boy." I smiled back. He continued, "You and me, why, er, we made a pretty good team together, don't you think?" I gave him a nod. "Yeah, we got it done, didn't we?" Then he added, "We work pretty good together; why don't you and me be partners"?

I couldn't speak, but my thoughts raced. Why would he think I would want to become partners with him? My God, we were as different as day from night. If I finished college, maybe I'd have a good future. What did he have ahead for him, except the next bottle of rot-gut?

If that were ever to happen, it's be no time before he stopped showing up for jobs. He'd be on a drunk for days. He probably lived in some dive room at the Railroad Hotel just by the tracks. He'd be spending Christmas day with a few bottles of Thunderbird or Ripple. I'd be opening presents by the fireplace with my family. But God, I didn't want to be mean to the man. "There but for the grace of God..." and all that. What could I say? I didn't want to be a shit.

Out came, "I guess I'll be needing to get back to school after the break."

He didn't say anything for a long time. Then he said, "Yeah, I guess you'll have to go your way, and I'll have to go mine."

I offered, "Can I drive you anywhere?"

"Nah," he said, "I think I'll just walk. Maybe I'll see you around," he added.

I nodded.

3
SETTLER OR PIONEER

FOLKS ARE EITHER settlers or pioneers—always have been, always will be. You are either one type or the other. "I'm staying put," or, "Time to get out of here." Here looks good, or there looks better. Yes, there are exceptions. Sometimes settlers become pioneers for a brief span of time. Sometimes pioneers settle down for a spell. But mostly, we're one or the other.

What an age we live in! So much wisdom to be received. The information highway comes right into our study. If you missed the newsflash—you're black. We're all black in terms of DNA. It doesn't matter whether your skin is pasty white or not. You are black. Human life began, we know for a fact, in Africa. Adam and Eve (if you're a literalist) were chocolate, or we think so. Isn't that great! We vanillas are the result of migration. Skinheads, Nazis, white supremacists, sorry for the bad news. You're wrong, and nobody cares about your stupid ideas.

The story of migration, in its various degrees, or lack of migration, is a fascinating one, indeed. At every juncture, every crossroads, every circumstance, people made the decision to stay put or move. Some stayed. Some moved. The ones that moved went various distances. Then they either stayed or moved on with others or without. Some people are a journeying sort. The earliest historical data in the Old Testament talks about "A wandering Aramean was our father, Abraham" (around 1800 BCE).

The reasons for migration or staying put are many. Having food where we are may result in our staying. Not having food may result in our leaving. If there is "peace in the valley," we might stay. If Attila the Hun keeps pestering us, we may leave. As long as we're reasonably comfortable, we often stay put. When we become very uncomfortable, we often pick up and leave. Fight or flee. Jews have been pushed out of just about every country on earth, as have other peoples.

So, we are settlers or pioneers, farmers or explorers, dwellers or campers, residents or nomads, those who stay put or those who journey.

In the book/film *Poseidon Adventure,* this issue is explored. The ship *Poseidon* turtles and flips upside down. The choice is to stay put and wait to be rescued by others, or help themselves and head out through an unknown path to the air above. They could stay and wait, or they could leave, thinking that the better choice. There are interesting arguments pro and con, concerning staying or going. In the story, about half of them stay and about half sally forth. No spoiler alert here about how it ends. But the story shows who we are. We are people who are inclined to stay put, or we are people inclined to move on.

As you review your life, how do you understand yourself? Have you moved multiple times and lived in many different places? Or are you in the same town you were born in, perhaps living in the same house as your parents? Are you a "home-boy," or a "No grass grows under your feet"? Have you traveled to many parts of the world or have you seen the next county over and that's about it? Our world needs both types. It always has and always will.

4

HIGH ON WHAT IS

IT'S NOT THAT I don't indulge in the occasional gin and tonic, highball, or Moscow Mule. I do occasionally. I also like those little gummy things, but I've only had three my entire life. So, I'm certainly not dependent on marijuana or other drugs.

I must be a little different, maybe a lot so. Seems I can get high on what is.

I just look around and I see some things that just about knock me off my feet. Wow and Shazam just can't describe it. Things that are more than impressive, stuff that is more than rad or boss or even far out.

Take, for example, a beetle. I don't know his scientific name. He and she live down in the Amazon rainforest somewhere. There was a whole long TV segment about this beetle on PBS, with film footage out of this world. Imagine this beetle about the size of a ladybug, just strolling along a leaf stem somewhere. Then, it is attacked by an ant. Ants are bullies, you know. They're strong, really strong. I've seen ants picking up great big sticks and stones and carrying them around like they were toothpicks or grains of sand. Ants are down to Planet Fitness almost every day, pumping iron and burning muscle.

The incident was all caught on film. An ant attacking this

little beetle, just minding his own business. I guess the truth is these ants really like the belly meat of this particular species of beetle. But film footage shows that as soon as the beetle gets jumped, it lowers itself down upon the leaf, and try as it may, the ant cannot flip the beetle over and enjoy lunch. The ant struggles and struggles to turn the beetle. Never happens. The ant moves on. When it's safe, the beetle moves on.

This scientist and filmmaker wasn't satisfied with just filming this. He asked, "How was this possible?" He pondered, "How can this beetle be so much stronger than the ant?" The beetle was one-half the size of the ant, and the beetle doesn't lift weights down at Planet Fitness (that we know of, anyway).

So, in comes research. The scientist observed that when the beetle is attacked, he secretes a fluid on the pads of his six tiny feet. Imagine an elephant with those big flat feet, only on the beetle, many times smaller. The beetle secrets a fluid between the bottom of his feet and the surface of the leaf, and the ant can't turn him over. Why?

Imagine two flat hard surfaces, perhaps two pieces of hard plastic or smooth metal. Put water in between these two surfaces and push them together and see what difficulty you have separating the two plates. If you've experienced this in the lab, perhaps you were impressed. That's the defense mechanism of the tiny beetle.

But the scientist didn't leave it at that. He invented an instrument to measure just how strong that beetle had become by secreting that fluid. He invented a contraption, and to understand the degree of the strength, imagine this. Imagine that a human being has six legs and is walking around like the beetle. Now imagine attaching six grand pianos to the bottom of each of those six feet. That is how much weight the ant has to overcome to flip over the beetle. Imagine that we humans would not be able to lift one grand piano, but six grand pianos! We cannot do this, but the little beetle in the Amazon has this much relative strength at his disposal.

Can you get high on this? I can. Holy cow! That is impressive. This is mind-blowing. It is incredible, which means beyond credibility, beyond belief. This is indeed a "Wow." I get high on these things. I get high on the things that are right in front of us.

A learned man, somebody who really understands the numbers, once said, "There are more stars in the heavens than all the grains of sands in all the oceans of our world." This statement should make you pass out cold. How many grains of sand is that? I live by a beach, a seven-mile beach. There's a lot, a whole lot of sand there. This is just one beach in one town in one country. There are millions of beaches in our world, each holding lots and lots of sand. This doesn't even account for all the sand at the bottom of lakes, seas, oceans, rivers. Can we even begin to get our minds wrapped around how much sand there is in our world? Then, this chap says, "There are more stars in the heavens than there are grains of sand in all the oceans of the world." Where are the smelling salts? We should be out cold on the floor. There's a word that comes to mind: AWESOME. We become overcome with AWE. Truth is, this information does more for me than an evening of Moscow Mules. My fingers are tingling as I type this.

Years ago, in Great Britain, they decided to put in a major highway. This resulted in their digging up quite a distance of some ancient Roman roads which were built more than 2,000 years previously. They carted off the stone to the British National Museum, and were so busy preserving antiquities that they didn't get back to the road-building for many months. When they returned they discovered that a number of plants had begun to sprout from the soil that was under the Roman-laid stones. This, in and of itself, is remarkable. What is even more remarkable is that there were several plants of various grasses and weeds that had gone extinct over the years in Great Britain. A variety of seeds were now growing again.

Seeds that lay dormant for 2000 years were growing again! How can this be?

The whole study of hibernation is under review. It used to be thought that various species of plants and animals either hibernated or they did not. Modern research is discovering that it's not either/or, which is to say, some species hibernate for days or weeks, awaken for a while, then re-hibernate. Others have various patterns to slow down the heart rate and breathing. One variety of weasel becomes impregnated in the fall, but the fetus does not grow. If it did, the mother weasel would lose too much of her body's energy feeding the fetus, and she would probably die before spring. But she is able to put the fetus into a suspended state until she can eat the needed food so that they can both survive.

The wonders and opulence of nature abound. Submersibles can dive about two miles and ROV's (remote operational vehicles) up to three miles. That's only halfway down into the deepest of oceans. But already they are discovering hundreds and thousands of new life forms which scientists never thought could survive at such extreme depths. What will they find when they can descend another three miles to the deepest of depths?

I once had a close encounter. No, not with a UFO, but with a spider. It was close in the sense of extended and intimate. I was in a building on the 7th floor, mesmerized by a spider outside the building weaving a web in the cold of autumn under a stiff north breeze. It was a fascinating experience. The wind was blowing the web and the spider here and there under tremendous force. Still it worked, doing what it had to do to survive.

It was not a large spider. Its body was no larger than a pencil's eraser and with those skinny little legs. I began to reflect. That spider has within it the same life force and the same basic equipment as I have. It has a tiny little heart that beats and beats. It is certainly shaped differently than a human heart, but it circulates oxygenated blood also. It has many eyes to see and a mouth to eat. It has legs that bend. My legs bend. Everything needed to survive and be alive was in that little pencil-eraser-sized spider. What does a spider's brain look like? How does it work? Then, my mind traveled to microscopic creatures, googleplexes of little tiny life forms. I'm high again.

Astonishing things abound. The miraculous is right under our noses. The unbelievable is happening moment by moment. Dare I use the word "miracles"? Ours is a world filled with glory. Yet we often slog along like drones, letting all there is to experience pass us by.

I suppose we all have our escapes. We try to get away from the world so we can just have some peace. Yet I find that I often get higher digging deeply into this gift called life. What wonders!

5

PORCUPINES

IT WAS THE coldest winter ever. Many animals of the forest died because of the cold. They froze to death. The porcupines, considering the situation, decided to group together to benefit from each other's warmth. They understood that only by coming together and sharing their warmth could they all survive the winter.

But as they huddled, their quills poked into each other, drawing blood, causing pain and discomfort. All of them were so uncomfortable that they began to distance themselves one from another. But then, they were cold again. It became a choice. They could either live alone in the cold and possibly die, or they could come together, be warmed by each other, but endure a prickly pain.

Wisely, they began to huddle together again. They were warmed by the others' closeness. They learned to live with the little pricks and pokes they received from others. They survived the coldest winter ever, together.

Human friendships do not bring together perfect people. Human relationships, like those of the porcupines, involve learning to live with the imperfections of others. The moral of the story above is – learn to live with the pricks in your life.

There is another good teaching story about the man who

sat in front of the cold fireplace on a chilly winter's night. The fire had gone out. There were not even embers on the hearth. The man sat in his chair, angry that he was so cold. He began to shout at the fireplace. "Give me warmth. Burn so that I will not be cold." Of course, the fireplace did nothing. The man didn't do anything either, except to continue yelling at the fireplace. "Oh, you're a worthless thing. What good are you? Why were you created if not to give warmth? Give me heat on this cold winter's night, or I shall surely die." That he did.

In human relationships, there are those who behave this way. They expect to be warmed but will do nothing to effect it. "I need to be warmed. But why won't others warm me?" They are like the porcupines who isolate themselves from the very sources of heat which they desire.

John Donne gave the thought, "No man is an island unto himself." Yet there are many indeed who elect to try to live without warmth, without friendship.

There are as many excuses as there are grains of sand in the oceans.

- There is something wrong with those others.
- It is their fault I am not warm.
- I have encouraged others to fetch my wood, but they do not.
- You see I am unable to get warm.

It is like the proverbial person who repeats a behavior over and again and expects different results. In their hearts, are they too proud? Nah. They are too lazy or stupid. Darwin did teach about the survival of the species.

There are reality checks in each of the above two stories. In the story about porcupines, the truth is that we are all pricks. Yet we can also all give warmth. It is not just we who are being pricked. We prick others as well, mindfully and ignorantly.

Take it up with the Creator why it is this way. Nevertheless, we must work with it. Prickly people in a prickly world, all needing warmth.

The man before the cold fireplace should teach us that warmth doesn't just appear. We must exert some effort. We have to rise from our chairs, haul in the wood and kindling, light and stoke the fire.

Perhaps, too, there is even a larger lesson to receive for those who have ears to hear and are wise enough to receive.

WE DIE ALONE.
WE LIVE TOGETHER.

6

TREES

"I THINK THAT I shall never see, a poem lovely as a tree."
Nearly every one of us has heard the beginning of this poem written by Joyce Kilmer. Are we familiar with the other five stanzas?

> "A tree whose hungry mouth is prest,
> against the earth's sweet flowing breast.
> A tree that looks at God all day,
> and lifts her leafy arms to pray.
> A tree that may in summer wear,
> a nest of robins in her hair.
> Upon whose bosom snow has lain,
> who intimately lives with rain.
> Poems are made by fools like me,
> but only God can make a tree."

Joyce Kilmer was not a woman as the name might imply, but a man, born Alfred Joyce Kilmer into a devout Roman Catholic family in New Brunswick, New Jersey in the year

1886. Joyce served in World War I in the 69th infantry in France and was killed by a sniper's bullet in 1918. He was thirty-one years old and left behind a wife and five children.

Poets do two things before they write. They notice, then they engage. There are millions of stimuli in life. We often see them but don't really see them. They go by unnoticed. We slog along here and there and most times don't see, hear, smell, taste, or touch much of anything. But suddenly, to the poet, something jumps out before him, and it says, "Hey, take a look at me." That thing is then noticed. It enters into the poet's life in a more significant and profound way than before.

Then, that which is noticed is engaged, and a dialogue begins. Poets take whatever the subject matter might be and reflect upon it with searching thought. It is like a conversation, even if no words are exchanged. There is a give-and-take, sharing with the subject matter. Whatever is noticed begins to teach the observer about itself. The process is intimate.

Some have never noticed a tree or engaged a tree. Joyce Kilmer did. It is hard to know what struck him to notice, any more than we know why certain things and experiences draw our attention. Joyce Kilmer became a friend to a tree and trees.

Twenty-nine percent of the earth is land. Of that land, thirty percent is forested. There are a lot of trees out there to notice and to engage.

Perhaps it was a quaking aspen that got Kilmer's attention. Perhaps the tree's leaves were happily dancing in the breeze. Perhaps he was taken by a particular fruit a tree bore. Perhaps it was a willow that seemed to be weeping. Perhaps the tree was unusually shaped. Perhaps it just gave him cool and shady rest on a hot summer's day.

I once knew a woman who would stand under a favorite tree. It was shaped almost like an umbrella. She would stand under the canopy of this tree for lengthy periods of time. When she was troubled, she would go to this tree and experience warmth and safety under the branches. It was her comfort tree, a healing tree.

Trees have a lot in common with human beings. At the very least, trees and humans are both alive, and trees and humans will someday die. It's interesting that when we humans die, we place our dead in wooden boxes made from trees, while trees simply topple over and lie at the feet of their forest friends. There they do their decomposing above the ground, not like us humans, who do it underground.

Humans have veins and arteries that transport blood. Trees have phloem and xylem that transport nutrients through sap, their lifeblood.

Trees suffer injury as we humans do. Branches break off and fall to the ground. People lose arms, legs, fingers, and toes. We refer to people as having limbs. Do trees have arms? I'm reminded of the talking trees in *The Wizard of Oz* who became angry with Dorothy when she picked some fruit. Trees were standing with their limbs bent as a human might with the hand to the waist, indignant at the offense.

As humans get sick and recover, trees become ill and recover. Naturalists have studied an interesting phenomenon in the forest. An illness, perhaps a blight, will begin in one part of a forest, then travel though the forest, but then stop. They have discovered that the unaffected trees create antibodies to resist the oncoming illness. Then they tell the other trees to do the same. It's a vaccination of sorts. It is communication that occurs among the trees. Perhaps it occurs through the leaves or the underground roots; they are not entirely sure. Conclusion: Like humans talk, trees talk.

Some trees live alone, and some people live alone. But most trees live in forests, as most people live in towns and cities. There are often clusters of like trees: white birch, elm, red maple, oak. There are often clusters of humans in neighborhoods: Polish, Chinese, Greeks, Sudanese. Mostly we find the same trees together and the same tribes of humans together. But we can find a beech tree among the sycamores, and a Russian among the Swedes.

As trees in a forest grow, their roots become entangled with each other as they penetrate the soil. This event gives each tree a stronger foundation than each would have alone. Together, trees can withstand the attack of strong wind and weather, while the lone tree may tumble, fall, and die. Likewise, when humans live in communities, we become deeply rooted with each other. We develop common history, language, culture, religion, purpose. When we are networked together, we are strong and protected by each other. We nurture and support each other.

People get around and always have. Researching our ancestry's DNA reveals that virtually all of us are a mix of cultures, histories, and countries. Trees get around, too. We humans walk. Tree seeds travel by wind. Their seeds travel in the fur of animals or may be excreted in scat far from where the seed was ingested, and there give birth to a new tree.

Trees protect themselves by wrapping themselves in bark. Humans wrap themselves in skin.

Most trees grow vertically. They grow straight and tall. There are trees that are bent over and twisted. Humans mostly grow upward—that is, vertically. We grow straight and tall. But there are bent-over and twisted humans as well. An interesting side note—today, it is still possible to see trees bent over in the forests. Native Americans often marked trails by bending a several-feet-tall sapling and tying it to the ground, forming an arch. These arches grew to be tree markers showing a route among the trails.

Some trees are very old. In the white mountains of California there is a Great Basin bristlecone pine tree named Methusaleh which is over 4,850 years old. Naturalists believe there are even older trees in the area which may date to 5,070 years. Its year of germination would have been about

3050 BCE. Other trees don't live many years at all. The acacia or wattles tree of Australia survives only six to twelve years.

The largest tree in terms of cubic feet is the General Sherman in California's Sequoia National Park, which stands some 275 feet tall. However, the General Sherman is not the tallest. That honor goes to Hyperion, another redwood in the California forests which ascends to just under 380 feet. Which is the shortest tree? This is a difficult question, especially if one considers the human-manipulated bonsai trees.

Trees are tall, short, fat, skinny. People are tall, short, fat, skinny. Trees and people come in all colors and strengths. Joyce wrote,

> "a tree whose hungry mouth is prest
>
> against the earth's sweet flowing breast."

He sees a tree suckling from the earth as a human baby would from its mother. Joyce continues,

> "a tree that looks at God all day,
> and lifts her leafy arms to pray."

Did he engage a tree whose lofty leaves and branches swayed back and forth, as many humans do with their arms as they pray? Certainly, Kilmer has personified, perhaps humanized trees.

> "A tree that may in summer wear
> a nest of robins in her hair.
> Upon whose bosom snow has lain,
> who intimately lives with rain."

He attributes human behaviors and traits to trees. He

understands that we are similar, related. His poem ends in a powerful climax.

> "Poems are made by fools like me,
> but only God can make a tree."

Joyce has not only noticed and engaged; he has knelt and worshipped. His encounter with trees not only became intimate; it became ethereal, spiritual.

> "I think that I shall never see,
> A Poem lovely as a tree."

7

FLOATING FREE

Written by friend Angus Watkins (2005)

LARSON CALLS WHEN summer is done, for the waters have cooled and the lake is ready for us now that most cottages are closed, and cabin cruisers swaddled in plastic on shore with crowds gone back to the city, dragging their jet skis and ATV's.

In ten minutes, my boat is uncovered, hooked up, and hauled out of its neglect from the barn. What minnows are left I scoop wriggling from a bait shop tank, together with a carton of crawlers freed of lethargy in a fridge, then hum up the highway that runs past a bridge, ending where water begins.

Larson waits at the landing with gulls on his shoulders, three poles in a hand, rod tips jiggling in expectation. I back down the ramp to launch that moment waters lift our craft from its cradle, so with it we bob and float free.

A congregation of big perch assembles twelve feet beneath us at the edge of some weeds, ready late afternoon to take in what might shimmer or gleam in lines we drop on them. They rise from muddy pews, a throng lifted from a last supper, offered on the altar of our hunger to engage mystery and eat. As the motor planes us home on the satin sea of Chautauqua Lake under a lapis lazuli sky somewhere between a summer sunset and autumn in our lives, we recall the ballast each of us has been to the other over years, sounding deep and dim holes where the soul swims.

Come spring, Larson plans to pull up his anchor and climb down from the pulpit after more than thirty years, having hurled lines and his heart in that craft. Many were caught up in what gleams. Untangled from the weeds and years, he'll bob and float free.

8

PROVERBS

WHAT IS A proverb? It's defined as a general truth. It's common knowledge, the stuff we all agree upon to be pretty much true. However, asserted truths sometimes contradict one another. Seemingly, what is the opposite of another truth is not falsehood, but sometimes, another truth.

Some early written proverbs come from 700 BC in the book of Proverbs in the Old Testament of the Bible. Others date earlier. Over the years, thousands of proverbs have been penned as expressions of general truth. People observe and study life, arrive at truths, then pen them into short, pithy sayings.

Proverbs seemed to be more popular years ago than they are today. Yet there are proverbs uttered by modern society as they were in ancient times.

Parents use proverbs to teach their children. They are like a catechism of common knowledge. Children, being innocent, and ignorant (meaning—not knowing) need to know truth if they are to function best as years go by. Yet many a child has to learn from the school of hard knocks, as they didn't listen well to their parents.

Take for example the proverb, "A stitch in time, saves nine." This saying came from the age of mending clothes, darning socks, sewing tears in fabric to make them last longer. Today we just throw clothing away. Years ago, we repaired it.

A stitch in time comes from the observation of the fraying and unraveling of threads. If these problems are taken care of sooner rather than later, the amount of sewing and stitching is less. If it's not tended to, a small hole in the sock becomes a bigger hole requiring much more work to mend.

So, this becomes a truth that can be used to apply to any number of situations. Paint the house now before the paint has peeled off so much that the wood deteriorates. Put on the new roof now, before it leaks, or at the first sign of a leak. Follow the servicing guidelines for maintenance of a vehicle, or pay larger repair bills later. Wash dishes immediately after a meal, as by waiting, food dries and more effort is required. Clean the house now before insects invade and you must pay for costly fumigation. Pay your bills now and avoid high interest rates on borrowed money and loans. Better a stitch now, than nine later. Better early a day than late a day. Better take control of the bear, or the bear will take control of you.

Young people often don't believe all this. Why? Because they have not had enough experience to confirm the truth. They often don't believe their parents' or teachers' instructions. They push a healthy and helpful proverb into the realm of platitudes. "Oh Mom, oh Dad, you've told me that a hundred times; what you say is not true." I personally have always found it very curious that youth can believe they know more than the aged who have decades more experience. Such is often the way.

Which leads to "You can lead a horse to water, but you can't make him drink." That is true of horses. It becomes a truth for humans as well. We lead our children to wells of refreshing water, life- sustaining water, but they do not drink. They stand there in defiance. Personally, I think the proverb would have been a little more accurate if the word "jackass" were substituted for horse. It drives the point home a little better for those who are mule-headed.

Some proverbs are very similar to other proverbs. For example, "A stitch in time saves nine" is strikingly similar to "The early bird gets the worm." Worms come up from the deep ground to enjoy the dewy grasses of nighttime. They are often slow to crawl back into their holes come dawn. When birds sing before sunrise, there is a reason. Their songs can roughly be translated to "Breakfast is ready; breakfast is ready." Down from the trees they go to the ground where they can actually hear worms move. Indeed, the early bird gets the worm. The bird who sleeps late, after a hard night partying, will get up late and miss the breakfast call.

Two more proverbs are very similar. "A chain is only as strong as its weakest link," and "A rotten apple spoils the barrel." There was a time, when upon entering the general store, one found the apple barrel front and center. The shopper would select apples, then pay. It is a fact indeed, that if an apple begins to rot and it is in close contact with another apple, the good apples will begin to rot as well. From one bad apple, a whole barrel of good apples could go bad. Similarly, chains are made of hundreds of links. If one link is defective and weak, in any way, it may break ruining the purpose of the entire chain. One bad apple. One weak link. I'm reminded of the many stories of burned churches due to arson. One misguided and twisted person with a torch can destroy an entire church building, as it were, and ruin the whole barrel. As a side note, most congregations rebuild their churches. It's in their character. But the idea is that it takes only one to damage and destroy so much. These are sobering proverbs.

"Discretion is the better part of valor" and "Flight, not fight" are twin proverbs too. What a strange age, that of pistol duels. "My honor has been offended, sir. I shall meet you with pistols in the field at dawn." Oh, they were brave and valorous men, they were. One of those men, filled with valor, ended up dead. What can be said of him? Perhaps "stupid" will work.

There is a legend in Erie, Pennsylvania known by many as Daniel Dobbins. He was an early merchant and sailor and sold his goods at the height of the War of 1812. This was the age of duelers and nearly everyone was (as is said today) "packing," meaning armed when traveling. Yet, Dobbins had more discretion than valor. He often got himself into arguments with men high on testosterone, eager to shoot anything or anyone. Dobbins had a better idea. He suggested the men step out behind the tavern and engage in an honest fist fight. Most, Dobbins won, as he was a big and strong man. A few he lost. Most importantly, he did not end up as a valorous dead man.

I suppose we admire the brave men of the Alamo who stood their ground and fought to the very last man. Their situation was hopeless, as was that of the Jews on top of Masada as the Romans built their ramp. The genius of the Jews is that they all took their owns lives in a suicide pact rather than be raped and tortured to death by the Romans. In some cases, fighting may be the best and only choice. But "flight" is a life option, and sometimes, maybe most times, the better choice.

"Beauty is in the eye of the beholder," and "One man's trash is another's treasure." Beauty and utility are relative commodities. It cannot be said of either that they are absolute. They become important only because a human being deems them important. A woman is beautiful if that woman has a least one other who believes she is beautiful. A work of art to one is not a work of art to all.

The great master's pieces of art are housed in thousands of museums throughout our world. By and large, they are beautiful treasures. But I think some are not, and you may think so as well. "They," that is "they" may think a certain work is beautiful and a treasure, and I may think it is trash.

For right or wrong, we judge. We select what our trash and treasures are, what we deem beautiful and what is ugly.

This whole subject slips into the realm of love. Which of us has not thought and perhaps even said, "I don't know what she sees in him?" Or "I don't know what he sees in her." Or "I don't know what he sees in him," etc. But they have found beauty in each other. To each other, they have become treasures.

There are so, so many good proverbs, pearls of wisdom to live by. One of my favorites by Ben Franklin, who penned many: "Early to bed, early to rise, makes a man healthy, wealthy, and wise." Late sleepers like to dismiss this one or tear it apart. I have found that it is mostly true. While there are those who are truly nocturnal, diurnals are much more successful, l think.

Monks wake at 4 a.m. Farmers wake at 4 a.m. Many are up and going out the door before the sun rises. They seem to be the healthy, wealthy, and wise. There seems to be a correlation.

I don't know how to explain these things. But there seems to be a correlation of long life to several factors. Churchgoing people live longer than non-churchgoing people. People with pets, mostly dogs and cats, live longer than those without. Those who live by oceans, rivers, and lakes have lower blood pressure. Those who read live longer. People do research and study and discover these things. Likewise, those who go to bed early (and we're talking 7 to 8 p.m. and up at 4 a.m.) seem to be healthier, wealthier, and wiser.

Don't believe me? Pull the blankets up and go back to sleep. You're not doing anything until noon. Right?

9

HEY, BLACKIE

MY CHILDHOOD FRIEND died recently. Her name was Jane. I knew her for sixty-five years. I knew her at a time when I didn't know that she was a girl, at a time when I didn't know that I was a boy. We were that young. All we knew was that we wanted to be friends, that we liked playing together. There was something else I didn't know.

She grew up and went her way and I went my way, leaving our little town in Nebraska to each live in several locations in the country. Since Nebraska, the closest we lived from each other was 500 miles. Yet we were able to maintain our friendship across the years and across the miles. We would find time, make time to keep in contact. We would write letters. We would talk on the phone. I met her daughter. She met my sons. We would physically visit each other. It was a sixty-five-year-old friendship, and I miss her dearly.

When we became adults, Jane had a favorite story she liked to tell about me. We would be with folks, and she would tell all her friends this favorite story. Maybe we would be at church or at a restaurant, or just gathered at her home.

On one occasion, my wife and sons were with Jane and me, and Jane started right in on her favorite story about me. It had to do with our walking home from school together way back then when we were childhood pals. We walked the same route and together because her home was not far from mine.

Every day, as we'd walk by this one home, a man, a mean-spirited man, would let out his dog. The dog was totally black. As the dog went running here and there, and we were clearly in sight, he would call out, "Hey blackie; hey nigger." I guess I must have thought that the dog's name was one or the other, maybe both. I didn't much care.

As a seven-year-old, I didn't make much of it. Adults were always saying things I didn't understand. Sometimes, in my mind, they said stupid things. This routine of letting the dog out and yelling happened just about every day. Maybe I didn't even notice that my friend, Jane, sort of looked away and dropped her head a little bit as we walked past this house.

As Jane used to love to tell the story, she said that I apparently got up on my high horse one day and sought to correct this misguided man. As Jane told it, I stopped in my tracks, put one hand on my hip and yelled out to that man, "Hey, mister, I just want you to know that Jane is not a blackie. She's a Brownie." I knew that about my friend Jane. She was a Brownie Girl Scout, not a blackie, and certainly not a nigger, whatever that was. Jane would smile each time she'd share this story about my naiveté.

I didn't remember this particular incident. But my friend Jane remembered it well. I think, upon my later reflection, that it was her way of complimenting my character, seeing something in me that I didn't even know was there.

I have marveled at my parents as I've thought back upon how my brother and I were raised. My father and mother were just the same way about this. Their belief and practice were simple. It didn't matter who we bought home from school or wherever else, they were all, every one, welcome in our home. Each and every one sat down with us at the kitchen table and shared a glass of milk and ate a few cookies. There was no judgement, no discrimination, no exclusion of any of our childhood friends.

Childhood is innocence. We're not born to hate others. We are taught to hate others. Left to our natural inclinations, we will make friends with whoever seems to be around us.

I did not know that Jane was a girl. I didn't know what a girl was. I did not know that Jane was black any more than I knew that I was white. She was a good friend. That was all I knew.

I think about that mean man who called out those mean words. It's hard to like a man like that. In fact, I think I hate him. I hate him because he tried to make me hate. He tried to make me hate my friend Jane. I have since learned that the people who use mean names like he did, hated my black girl friend Jane. He didn't know her. He never played with her.

I do hate that man. But I also pity that man. Few people these days use the Holy Bible to help direct their living, but I've seen some truths in that Book. Jesus' words are recorded in that Book, and he spoke some powerful words. One time he said this,

> If anyone causes one of these little ones who trusts in me to sin, it would be better for him if a large millstone were hung around his neck and he were thrown into the sea. – Mark 9:42

Trying to get another person to hate somebody is a sin, isn't it? Jesus wasn't very happy about people like that. I think that man must have had a very unhappy life to be filled with so much hate to do that mean thing, day after day after day.

Eventually, I came to understand that Jane was a girl and she was black. I came to understand that I was a boy and I was white. We both spent a lot of our adult lives trying to think the best about each other because this broken world put mean, hate-filled thoughts into our heads and the innocence was gone. But we still were friends, Jane and I.

I remember playing in the back yard with Jane. We would

run and run and run in circles. We'd fall down dizzy and laugh. We'd play on the lawn, sometimes in the dirt. We'd see ants and other bugs. We'd put our hands across our chests and lie out flat and roll down hills. We'd play until the sun started to set, when we had to go home. Jane was my friend. We played together, and I miss her.

10

THE IN-BETWEEN...OR NOT?

WE ARE ALL travelers. From birth to death, we travel between nothing and nothing.

Before birth there was no time. After death there is no time. Time exists only if there is life. We have life now, so we live in and with time. Before we are born and after we die, there is neither life nor time. Thus, from birth to death, we travel between nothing and nothing.

The thoughts above would be those spoken by many, perhaps most philosophers. A huge part of philosophy is epistemology, the study of how we know what we know. We cannot know before our birth. We cannot know after our death. Thus, there is nothing before our birth and nothing after our death. We can only know because we have life in time.

Those who buy into another thought realm and believe in some after this life existence, be it a form of reincarnation or resurrection, propose a different view.

They say, there may have been life and time before birth, and there may be life and time beyond death. They posit this enigmatic word, "eternity," that is that time has neither a beginning nor an end. Philosophers respond with "poppycock," as their world revolves around reason, whereas there are those others who revolve their lives around faith.

11

AUTHORITY

AFTER THE ID and ego, Freud designated the third element of the human personality, "the superego." It is the parent in us, the right and wrong in us, the "Don't do this – do that," in us. Superego is authority, which comes externally to us, usually through parents, then is assimilated into us as a self-governing authority. Some people mature to have high levels of internalized authority. Others care little about authority, having no restraints to thought or behavior. The police and prisons get to mind after those.

There is a no man's land, roughly the teenage years, when the superego is in between external authority and internalized authority. In this wilderness between youth and maturity, we are still learning rights and wrongs from external authorities and experience.

It is well to reflect upon our authorities and why we have selected them to govern our lives. Some authorities guide us in certain situations. Other authorities guide us at other times.

The parents, if there are any, are at the top of the list. They teach manners, behavior, courtesy, mores, and values. We have generally grown up assimilating most of our parents' qualities.

Teachers are next in line. Then the police, pastors, even peers. We allow them, each and all, to be our authorities or not. Should I walk across the street in the middle of the block? The external authorities say "No." That doesn't mean we will be obedient on most occasions, or ever. And so it goes.

Some people in authority don't really have authority. They don't have the qualities to be an authority. They may talk the talk, but don't walk the walk, and even a fool can see through that. A badge or uniform, stars, stripes, and large desks do not an authority make. So, these authorities are neither respected nor obeyed, however much they yearn to be.

Authorities have certain qualities that make them authorities. They are wise in their work. They are charitable. They are skilled. They are gifted, even charismatic. They may not necessarily be good. Archbishop Fulton Sheen once offered that wisdom is not necessarily virtuous; there are intelligent but evil men.

We need authority in the same way that sheep need a shepherd. Few are shepherds these days to know how very wayward sheep are. Sheep's tiny brains and behavior have gotten them into a peck of trouble at every turn. Without shepherds, sheep may have become extinct years ago. In many ways, we mortals need authority as well. Without authority, there is mayhem.

Who we allow to lead us politically has entertained humanity for years. We have not always selected wisely. Some might argue that there have been no good politicians, ever. These people are called by various names but get little done. They are mostly idealists and do little to better society.

It is odd to consider the great religious authorities of the ages who were humble, pious, self-effacing types. Best known in the Western world, perhaps, is Jesus, who demonstrated his authority by riding into the capital city on a donkey, and then getting crucified upon a cross. It's perplexing how his legacy continues. So very different from Pax Romana.

Are our authorities those who think and act just as we do? If so, how does that make them worthy to follow?

What is your litmus test? How do you know to whom to give your life over? As we sally forth through life and witness the endless stream of those who vie for power, how do we know who might be the better choice? The answer lies in fear. Follow not the fearless leader. Rather, follow the leader filled with fear. Those who pretend authority present themselves as loud and brash. They are arrogantly filled with themselves and little else.

An authority to give oneself over to should have fear in his or her eyes and be driven to the knees. They don't have to prove anything to you or to others. They know what they know. Their purpose is far too great to be mindful of ego any more. When called upon, they make a difference. They bring peace to chaos.

12

OLD-TIMER BENEFITS

ONCE OVER THE hill, the down run goes pretty fast. As we age, we deteriorate physically and mentally. We acquire stiff joints. Our muscles weaken. Our immune systems are not as strong, and metabolism slows. All sorts of illnesses and health problems come calling as we get older. Loneliness and isolation set in. Is it any wonder that seniors often suffer from depression? Further, suicide among the elderly is second only to that of teens. With the grim reaper just around the corner, seniors often feel like there's not much in the future to live for.

Yet being among the elderly affords benefits that are denied the younger. There are, indeed, many gifts we receive as we age. They are dividends earned. They are rewards for having survived the many ups and downs of long life. There are so many that I'll number them.

1. We do not lose the tickle factor. If you were ticklish when you were younger, you are just as ticklish when you are older. I'm sure there's a scientific study on this somewhere. From my research of many, I believe this to be true.

2. What do seniors have that the younger don't? In a word, we have Medicare. Medicare is a huge incentive to stay alive, so you can walk in and out of the doctor's office and never

reach for your wallet or purse. Young people don't have Medicare. We do.

3. We have discounts. When you reach that magic age of sixty, you will become a member of the American Association of Retired People, a name so long it was shorted to AARP so old folks could remember it. In the magazine you receive regularly you will read about dozens, in fact scores of discounts from this store and that hotel, this restaurant and that service. You can often tell a senior, even if they look young and have colored their hair black, as they are often overheard saying, "Give me my damned discount!"

4. Volunteering is another benefit of aging. During the work years, one returns to the homestead exhausted and worn, far too tired to be a den mother or soccer coach. Sure, some do try. The point is, in retirement you have sixty to eighty more hours each week available because you're not working, so you can volunteer time to any number of worthwhile organizations.

5. Once you are old, you can speak your mind. No more need you bite your tongue and not say what you're really thinking. Imagine during your work years saying to your boss, "Oh, bugger off." You could kiss that job goodbye. Once retired, you can say that to everybody. If somebody ticks you off, just let it spew out like Old Faithful. Rarely is an older person beaten up just because they speak their mind.

6. There's something young people seldom do...take bus trips. Seniors are going here and there in great hordes, visiting this museum and that tourist destination. It was on a bus trip that I finally learned all the words to a great song. That was after several bottles of wine went through the coach on the journey back home.

"Show me the way to go home.

I'm tired and I wanna go to bed.

I had a little drink about an hour ago;

and it went right to my head."

Old people sing that on a bus much better than young people ever could.

7. This next benefit is primarily for older men; however, it could apply in some cases to women. The benefit is zippers. Yes, we have them when we're younger, but they're generally not needed with aging. Older men have to go so frequently that they're often seen walking around with their pants zippers down. Most young people attribute this to the feeblemindedness of the aged. Not so. We simply reason as follows. We're just going to have to zip down in a few minutes anyway, so why bother? And also, there's much less to showcase and nobody is interested anyway. Old people leave their zippers down. No problem. A younger man with his zipper down might get hit with a purse to the head, or possibly arrested for indecent exposure.

8. The next benefit has to do with our accumulation of money. During our working years, we scrimp and save, pinching pennies and worrying, "Will we ever have enough?" There are fools in the world who never give a thought to the future, but many older folks are sitting on a fair pile of savings. Right now, the baby boomer generation has more wealth than any other American generation ever. We have money, and everybody wants it, especially drug companies and nursing homes. Most seniors are instead spending it on all-inclusive vacations, cruises, marijuana, and cougars.

9. The day I retired I took one item of my apparel and disposed of all of them, save one. I took every one of those devil-created neckties and threw them in the trash. I saved one to

be buried with, but I may toss that one as well. How many years we worked with a hangman's noose tied around our necks, just because fashion dictated? Insanity. If you see an older fella still traipsing around with a necktie on, he just hasn't gotten the word. Psychologists call it "denial." You're retired, buddy. Get rid of that awful thing!

10. The next benefit has to do with why grandchildren are referred to as "grand." When we had our own children, we had to keep them. That's part of the deal with parenting. You make them, you keep them. Grandchildren are another thing. They are fun to visit and play with, but we can leave grandkids. They are the responsibility of parents, not grandparents. So, little known to most who are younger, as Grandma and Grandpa are driving home, surely one will blurt out to the other, "Isn't it grand that those kids aren't ours?"

11. The next benefit is that the chains to the desk have been broken. Our noses are no longer "to the grindstone." We are no longer "working nine to five." The time clock is gone. We are now free to move about, and that we do. That daily grind is gone. Do you know how you can tell a senior? There's a three-question test. (1) What time is it? (2) What day of the week is it? (3) Why did I come in here? The senior will score a perfect, "I don't know." This number 11 might be summarized by the word "freedom."

12. The next benefit is that you can wear the same clothes for several days, even many days. There's this miracle product you can get in the market called "Febreze." Use it if flies start to follow you. The point is, you can dress up or you can dress down. You can wear stripes with plaids, and paisley with corduroy. Older women are often seen in public with just one earring. (Well, not just one earing. They have clothes on, too.) Nobody ever comments on how an

older person is dressed. If it's some weird looking hobo-type, pajama-wearing fella, folks just walk by thinking, "Another old man."

13. Once you are retired you will never again have to endure a job performance evaluation. Remember sitting across from that jerk and squirming as he/she asked awful questions about what you did with your time? Remember leaving the interview feeling so worthless and knowing you would receive neither a raise nor a bonus? No more. You can take this job and, well…we all know how that ends.

14. Another of the many benefits of being an old-timer is you learn to say this wonderful two-letter word: NO. Do you want to babysit the grandkids tonight? No. You want to live in a nursing home, don't you? No. Well, then, come and live with us. No. Can we come for a visit? No. Do you want to serve on x,y,z committee? No. Don't you want to teach Sunday School? No. Don't you think you should change your clothes sometime? No. Shouldn't you eat more than toast and coffee? No. Don't you think you should go see the doctor? No.

    Get out of my house. *Wheel of Fortune* is about to start.

15. Next, misbehaving becomes a primary form of entertainment. Who is allowed to act up as a child? Here comes the spanking. School is just another word for prison. The uniforms are so the same. Step out of line and get detention. The work years are nothing but obedience. Once you are older, you can misbehave all the time and get away with it. What's the punishment, ever? Nothing. There are some great misbehaving games, especially with one's children who are forever trying to please their older parents. But we old-timers know that the last years are the "payback years." Those kids put us through hell getting them raised. Now, we're going to give it to them before we cash out.

16. Remember how seriously you took everything when you were younger? Everything was a crisis, a catastrophe. OMG! OMG! You name it. We were wired. We got offended easily. We pouted. We got angry. We mounted the high horse of righteous indignation. An old-timer simply doesn't have the energy to do any of that anymore. It's been proven that being silly and indifferent are much more energy efficient. Old people (who can get beyond that depression thing) are the happiest age group ever. Old people read *MAD Magazine*. "What, me worry?" While everyone else who is younger is running around shouting that the world is coming to an end, we know better. We've seen the world try to do that many times and fail. We're pretty sure the sun will come up tomorrow.

17. Let look at the next three benefits together: imagination, creativity, anticipation. It's not that younger people don't have these, but that we still have them also. Imagination: Our minds take us on wonderful journeys through memory. Creativity: Grandma Moses started her painting at age seventy-eight. Anticipation: We still get excited. Heavens, most of us have our coats on and are ready to go out the door a full four hours before our doctor's appointment.

18. The body may be decreasing, but the spirit may be increasing. Enough said.

19. Old-timers still have urges. The desire to do is still there. To live is to urge. We still want things and long for things. While blood still flows within us, we feel the promptings. The kissing cousin to urge, by the way, is hope. While there is life, there is hope.

20. This has become a rather long list of old-timer benefits. There are many more, I am sure. For many, a benefit is the laying aside of theological angst. We ponder our whole lives the larger questions of God, destiny, life beyond

death. Life is a faith journey. Little is actually known. Almost everything about existence has to do with faith—that the earth will maintain its orbit and the sun rise is a faith statement. It could be that it stops tomorrow. Who can know for sure? But the old-timer can and often does lay all this worry to the side as the days and hours become fewer. At best, it's a guess or a bet. Who can know? But whereas the younger will toss and turn over these questions, the old-timer can arrive at some semblance of peace, of acceptance of whatever comes.

13

DEEP CALLS TO DEEP
Written by Ben Larson-Wolbrink (2020)

THERE'S A BLUR of clover under my bare feet as I race toward the water. I'm around seven years old, and we have just arrived at our family cottage on Lake Pymatuning in western PA. Just like last visit, and every time before that, I'm off and running. No matter how early in the season—or how cold the water is—I can't wait to take the plunge.

My heart is pounding. I'm aiming my toes for bare patches of grass between the clover and the honeybees lurking on their flowers. These leaps make my pace erratic, but they don't slow me down. Maybe—just maybe—I won't get stung this time....

No matter how many times grownups tell me to put sandals on—and no matter how many times I get stung (which is just about every time)—I keep running.

I can't help it. I'm drawn to water.

In his book *Flute Solo*, Matthew Kelty writes, "Water is always an invitation to immersion, an immersion with a quality of totality, since it would accept all of me, as I am. Some primal urge invites me to return whence I came (117)."

Have you ever had one of those moments where you catch a glimpse of water mid-air? Once, I watched waves on Lake

Michigan slam into a break wall, hurtling masses of water straight upwards. At first, I was compelled by the power of it, reveling in the deep *whooshing* of sound and the jagged walls of water created after impact. But then, I found myself drawn to the precise moment one drop of water reached the apex of its journey—for a brief second—before returning back down under the pull of gravity.

Years later, in a season of my life when I felt like I was drying up in the desert of southern Arizona, I was speeding along a highway coming up, out of the mining town of Bisbee. Seemingly out of nowhere, a cloud opened in front of me, sending down huge droplets. Somehow, I was able to focus on one drop—again, only for a split second—before it splattered onto my windshield.

> *All streams run to the sea, but the sea is not full; to the place where the streams flow, there they continue to flow.*
>
> -Ecclesiastes 1:7

Before those distinct moments, each of those drops had traveled countless oceans, clouds, springs, and streams, and will continue to do so for as long as I can imagine. (Heck, it's even possible that they are the same drop.)

Eternity in a drop of water.

Water is as elusive as it is eternal. Just when I'm sure it's the power of the wave that draws me, I find eternity in a droplet. Just when I think it's the flow of the current or the pull of the tide, I discover the clarity of a still pool.

All the while, water is returning. And, all the while, it is drawing me to do the same.

14

THE THIN LINE BETWEEN A KICK AND A HUG

WHEN MY FATHER died, when I was fifteen, I was simply devastated for weeks. I cried day and night. Finally, I moved on but with an angry, volatile attitude toward everyone and the universe in general. I was mad, damn mad, because I was hurt, damn hurt.

Of course, I didn't understand this. I would just fly off the handle and shout and yell and run out of the house to be alone for hours. There were times I thought I was going mad. I was so unlike the person I used to be. I often wonder how I survived those years, that I didn't do something awfully hurtful to another, that I didn't self-destruct. My poor mother took the brunt of a lot of it, as my older brother was off at college.

One evening, Mom made me dry dishes as she washed. I was in no mood for that. I was banging pots and pans as I tossed them into their respective drawers. My protest was playing out in angry ways. Mom kept trying to work with me. You understand – like trying to get a raging bull back into its pen. Just then, as I was flailing about, I dropped a glass bowl onto the floor where it broke. It was not just a glass bowl, but her grandmother's glass bowl, one that she cherished, and I knew it.

I fully expected the slap to the head. It was a customary way of my mother working with me, the raging bull. She would come up behind me, and with an open hand, hit me on the back side of my head, sending my whole body forward. It happened so many times, I fully expected her response. I looked at her. She looked at me. I dropped my head and she took a step closer. Then she hugged me and said, "It was an accident. I know you didn't mean to do it." I burst into tears as she held me. "I'm so sorry, Mom. I'm so sorry." There were not any more words as we swept up the broken glass and finished off the rest of the dishes.

How did she know at that very instant what I needed most was not a kick in the arse, but a hug? It might have gone the other way, but it didn't. She knew that a kick in that moment would do no good. She knew that an understanding hug would be healing and make all the difference in the world.

> "For everything there is a season and a time for every purpose under heaven...A time to break down and a time to build up... a time to weep and a time to laugh."
> Ecclesiastes 3:1-8

There is a time for a hug and a time for a good swift kick to the arse. But how do we know when to do what?

Yes, there were times when I was spanked as a child—not excessively but necessarily. Children are born bull-headed and obstinate. Many don't respond to verbal reasoning. I was one who required—well, that my attention was secured.

A farmer was having a very difficult time getting his donkey to cooperate and do some work. In fact, the ass sat on his ass and would not budge no matter how hard the reins were pulled. A neighbor happened along and suggested that he had a solution. He took a thick branch and whacked the ass right on top on his nose. The ass got up and was ready to work. The neighbor commented, "Sometimes you just have to get their attention."

Actually, I'm sort of an expert on asses, having been called a horse's ass on more than one occasion. I do see the behavior similarities.

Of course, kicks in the arse are usually more figurative than literal. I have had so many; I hesitate to begin a list. Most were necessary. Some were excessive. Some were unjustified from my vantage point. Is one approach necessarily any better than another? Is a hug always better than a kick or a kick always better than a hug? No, they are each two separate tools in the box to be applied appropriately.

However, sometimes the point is lost. I remember very vividly staying after school one day and writing on the blackboard. I was in the third grade. I wrote a sentence over and over again. I remember the teacher sitting there glaring at me, administering her kick in my arse. By golly, she was going to teach me a lesson. The trouble is I can't remember the sentence I wrote. I can't remember the specifics of my crime against education. I can't remember why I had to write that one sentence over and over again. A good swift kick I did receive, but did it help me any? I can't be sure.

Grades are sometimes an arse-kicking. Of course, for the "A" students out there, not so much. But an "F" doesn't feel so good. In fact, "D's" don't feel so good either. Were they helpful in guiding me along to become a better student? "Here's your report card, Gary. You failed again." Ouch. Did I become a better student because of the kick?

Does a kick discourage or encourage? Does a hug discourage or encourage? Does a kick give us hope and inspire us? Does a hug give us hope and inspire us?

I was a weekly director at our church camp for years. It was a wonderful, loving environment, and I believe that even one week at camp had a positive effect on most of the kids who attended.

One night, in the middle of the night, our peaceful sleep was shattered with what sounded like a military invasion. It sounded like gun fire and more. It was fireworks. They went off here and there all around the camp. We didn't know they were fireworks immediately, so we were scared to death. The blessing was that all the kids were so exhausted from the day's fun they slept through the whole invasion. But all the adults and counselors were up, as the fireworks continued.

We could see older teens running around here and there, making mischief, having their fun. We need to catch just one, I thought to myself, and so we did. We actually ran one down and tackled him. As a couple of my larger counselors held him, he turned into a bowl of jelly. I yelled, "What in God's name are you doing, scaring my kids half to death?" He started to cry and said he was sorry.

We put him in a room with a bunch of us. And so it began. With him sitting right there, we talked through our many options. "Shall we call the police right now? Who are your parents? Wait until they hear about what you did tonight? Do you know the other guys who were involved in this?" He was a wreck, instantly repentant. We could see he wasn't a bad boy, just a good boy who did a bad thing.

Who knows where these ideas come from, but the cook came up with a plan.

> So, look here, fella, you are in a peck of trouble. This little war game you played at the expense of our camp could ruin your life forever. The police will lock you and your friends up and throw away the key. Or... you can come to dinner at camp tomorrow night and sit and eat with the campers. Do you know all the guys who were involved in this? Then, you need to contact every last one of them. Every last one of them needs to be at this camp tomorrow night for supper. Do you understand? Will you do this?

He agreed faster than a kid could open a birthday gift. The next night, twenty teenage town boys arrived and had dinner with fifty campers and staff. We didn't say anything about the event. No lectures. We let the experience teach, and I think it did.

Our camp was never attacked by bored town teenagers again after that. While nobody came back to talk to us later or apologize or thank us for not telling their parents, I've always believed we made an impact, one much more powerful than if we'd administered a kick in the arse. I often wonder how those boys turned out. It was what some refer to as a teachable moment, and just maybe we got the point across.

How do we know when to do what? I write this in the midst of the George Floyd national protests. A man wearing a police uniform put handcuffed George Floyd to the ground, and then indifferently put his knee to his neck for nine minutes, ignoring calls of, "I can't breathe." He killed George Floyd in cold blood right on camera.

The United States of America is responding, "No more hugs." This country needs a good swift kick in the arse, and that is what is happening. Protests are happening in every major city in the nation. A call to end police brutality, the indiscriminate killing of blacks and people of color, to end a systematically unjust system for many in this country. God, let us listen to the cries, please. Prayers and patience and forgiveness have not worked. Racism is systemic, deep-seated. Our collective arse needs to be kicked and kicked hard. We all should be uncomfortable. Change, real change, must occur.

On the other hand, what did Germany and Japan need at the end of World War II? Some more arse-kicking? No. The world community responded with ways to help rebuild. This is not to say there were not political consequences to these countries. But when the war ended, it was time to build up, not tear down anymore. It was time to bury the hatchet and make peace. It was a time for the world to re-hug itself again, however difficult that might be.

After our Civil War, what did Lincoln do, after our country's most divided and bloodiest war ever? He sought to reconstruct, to reunify, to rebuild, to somehow honor the opposition in their defeat. It would not have been the right thing to push the noses of the Southern rebels into the mud. It would not have been the right thing to make them suffer any more. They were broken. They lost. It was time for the North to help repair the breach and heal a broken nation.

I marvel at the complexity of our international relationships throughout history. And it becomes even more complicated as the years roll along. In today's world, those who work in the area of diplomacy have their plates full. How to find the narrow path in each and every situation? It is not so easy as either/or. How do we deal with nations in the moment as they struggle to advance their interests and we ours? Those with simple answers do not provide answers. Turning belly-up, or "Bombing the hell out of them" are not answers, ever. It's hard enough to guess what to do in individual situations. National and international problem-solving is always a nightmare. Yet there are those who endeavor daily in the United Nations, in unions of various types, in peace agreements, in summits and negotiations. These are the people from every nation who are attempting to save our world. Bless their efforts.

Life is a paradox for sure. And this is just one more example of the many polarities in which we find ourselves. When do we give and receive the hugs? And when do we give and receive the kicks in the arse when they are needed?

In homes, in families, at work, at sports, at school, in all the myriad social gatherings that we become a part of, when is a hug the right thing and when is a kick the right thing? The line is thin, very thin indeed. President Lincoln was a brilliant man and left us a great deal of wisdom. On one occasion during the agony of our Civil War, he said, "I have been driven many times upon my knees by the overwhelming conviction that I had nowhere else to go." We make decisions many times each day that will affect others for good or ill. May we approach these occasions with humility and prayer.

15

BEYOND THE PAIN OF DEATH

MOM AND DAD were smokers. Dad more so than Mom. He'd knock off a couple packs of Lucky Strikes every day. Before we were aware of the harmful effects of cigarette smoke, I would show my love for my parents by buying each of them a carton of cigarettes at Christmas time.

Dad lived fully. As one of my friends bragged, "I work hard, and I play hard." Dad burnt the candle at both ends, as the old saying goes. He loved his beer, smokes, fishing, food, and who knows what other vices.

When he was forty-three and I was thirteen years old, Dad had a major heart attack. The doctor told him that if he could stop smoking for two years, he might go on to live many more years. I remember sneaking cigarettes into the hospital at my father's request.

He never stopped smoking. He didn't slow down a bit. Two years later, I came home from school to find a note from my mother who said she was at the hospital with Dad. I pretty much ran the six or seven blocks and got into his room just in time to see Dad take his last breath, at age forty-five. For this fifteen-year old, it was a crushing experience. As my mother, my dad's father, and I walked home, it felt numb, as if we were on some cloud, in another dimension. The foundation block of our being was no longer there in just one instant. We were dazed, trudging home, shell-shocked.

Then came a whirlwind of activity. People came to the house. The pastor visited several times. There was a funeral service and drive to the cemetery on a snowy February day. Then, everybody left. We were alone. We cried for days. My mother would fall into a heap on the floor and sob for hours. I cried, day and night. I couldn't stop for long. It went on and on and on. I'd go to sleep crying. I'd wake up crying.

Then, there was this idea that came crashing into my brain, this thought that stopped my crying in an instant. It came in the form of a question. "What would Dad think about me carrying on like this?" He would not like to see me crying every day, all the time. He would not want to know that I was unhappy. If there is a heaven, and Dad is looking down upon me, what would he want to see? He would want me to enjoy life as he had. He would want me to journey through life happily.

It was a turn-around, an about-face. I had been walking toward sadness. I turned and chose happiness. It sounds simple, but it truly happened to me. I felt I was at a crossroads. In my life I could go this way or that. I remember choosing. Everything did not change at once, but I remember thinking, "I will live the kind of life my father would have me live – a brave life, a full life, a happy life."

There would still be times, awful times. I was angry inside. I didn't understand what I was angry at, but I'd explode. Anybody near me received my anger, and I hurt so many, especially my mother. I'd run out of the house, down to the bay, jump in my small boat, row to the middle, and scream. But then, I'd come back and choose again to be happy. Over and over again, I'd choose to be happy. I do it, even now, many times each day.

Fifty-seven years have passed, and there are still times that I have outbursts of tears. I miss my father. I think about what life might have been like had he lived. But I think about this only briefly. It is what it is. I choose to be happy.

We never "get over the death of a loved one." We don't really move on. We don't assimilate death into life. We simply cope. That would be about as much as we might say about dealing with death – we learn to cope.

There are some who never stop falling in a heap onto the floor, sobbing over loss. My heart goes out to these. I wish they could find joy somewhere, anywhere.

I will not give death such power. I will kick and claw and scratch and flail against that old enemy until it finally takes me.

I personify and pretend. I think that I'm in conversation with death and I say:

> You're nothing. You will not control me, you slimy, rotten thing. You will not make me grovel before you. You cannot make me unhappy. I choose to be happy and spit in your face, you awful aberration of creation. You've knocked me down, a good punch. But look. I stand again and again. Your slings and arrows are nothing. Go away. Be gone. The day is here. I breathe.

The struggle continues between good and evil, between life and death, between joy and sadness. I think of my father and I smile. Remembering the pain of death does nothing to help me along. But the memory of Dad will pull me into the future.

16

CAMP DUFFIELD

(sing to the melody of "The Ash Grove")

Camp Duffield, Camp Duffield, sweet home of my childhood,
The old road leads up to the pond in the glade.
Camp Duffield, Camp Duffield, I see pine-green forests,
The fields and the meadows that our God has made.
In my mind, I see faces of old friends and new friends,
Of good times and tough times that helped me to grow.
I think of the mem'ries of Jesus' close presence.
As I think back on Duffield, I'm never alone.

Camp Duffield, Camp Duffield, The Spirit has moved me,
My call I see clearly through sunshine and rain.
Camp Duffield, Camp Duffield, to share with each other,
In living and in laughter, in joy and in pain.
Together in the warm mist, we're walking and talking,
The vespers' solemn singing still touches my heart.
Camp Duffield, Camp Duffield, sweet home of my childhood.
Your mem'ries are always with me. We're never apart.

17

LOVE NEVER ENDS

EVEN FOR THOSE unfamiliar with the Holy Bible, most have heard the phrase "love never ends." Perhaps they heard the idea in a song or read it in a poem. The phrase "love never ends" originates in the book of I Corinthians, chapter 13 in the New Testament Bible and that verse 8 reads, "Love never ends," sometimes translated "Love never fails," essentially the same concept.

John and Molly were high school sweethearts. They honored each other and were very much in love. They continued their relationship in college. They deepened their relationship in graduate school and were at last married. They were as happy as any couple could be. They began their first jobs. They bought their first home. Then Molly came down with a debilitating disease that, although it probably wouldn't kill her for years, nevertheless would make her a wheelchair-bound invalid. When John heard the news of the illness, he headed for the hills. He left and they were divorced quickly. John got remarried some years later. Molly remained single and was cared for by institutions.

Did John love Molly? No one can say what one might do in a similar situation. John didn't want to spend his live caring for an invalid wife. Did he stop loving her when he divorced her? Did he ever really love Molly?

Henry and Hilda were a young couple very much in love. It was an earlier age. They had immigrated to the United States as very young people. Their love also began in high school, and their courtship progressed as any other might. In this earlier day, in the early 1900s, young men and women did things together in groups, chaperoned as it were. Yet Henry and Hilda were falling in love.

Henry took a job that required traveling. He was overseas when he received the news that his Hilda had been run over by a team of horses pulling a wagon. She was in hospital. Henry cut short his trip. Hilda survived but one leg was broken in multiple places. Somehow the setting of the bones caused a severe bow in her leg, such that she used a walker the rest of her life. She would be an invalid and would need care. Nevertheless, Henry and Hilda went on to be married. He loved Hilda and she loved Henry.

Their life was not easy. Henry had to work. Hilda did the best that she could, pushing a walker around the house, bent over a vacumn sweeping the floor, or struggling to prepare the evening meal. Yet they had two children and were happy.

Henry lived to be quite old. Hilda, undoubtedly due to the earlier accident, had many problems in later life. She was dying in hospital, and Henry came daily to see her. Palliative care was unknown at this point. Henry would sneak in a small pill bottle of straight whiskey, and how Hilda would perk up in her bed to receive it. With the gentlest of hands, he would feed the "relief" to his love, and she would answer back with a smile.

Hilda died and Henry wept. Henry loved Hilda. Why did he continue to love Hilda when she had a debilitating accident? Why didn't Henry divorce Hilda as John had done to Molly? Henry could have chosen an easier life. Why didn't Henry stop loving Hilda and move on?

We might answer these questions in any number of ways. Both stories are certainly complicated and there are hundreds more details that might be understood in the playing out of each life story.

Explanations and complications away. It comes down to something very elementary, something basic, something true. Love never ends. It doesn't end because within the understanding of love is the strong idea of fidelity. Commitment or fidelity is a huge part of love.

Buy in or don't. Believe it or don't. Make it a maxim or don't. If one uses this idea as a building block of life, as a truth upon which to stack other truths and live consequently, then what is, is, what is.

John did not love Molly. Henry did love Hilda. John did not love Molly because what they thought was love ended. John left Molly. He never saw her again. How could he say that he loved Molly? One does not have love, then not have love. We can have a car and later not have a car. We can have money and later not have money. But we cannot have love and later not have love. Love never ends.

Henry loved Hilda. Hilda loved Henry. Their love never ended. Their love continued because it was love. There is no "off" switch, when it comes to love. There is no "failure" with love.

Does it end after this life? No one can really say. Some believe that love goes on into eternity. That is a pretty big jump from life as we know into a realm defined as eternity. We have difficulty understanding eternity. Does love never end in this life and in the life to come, if there is one? You may decide. I certainly can't tell you what to believe.

I do believe that we use the word "love" far too loosely. Love is a force that doesn't end. Or if it does end, what good is love? Is it nothing more than a passing passion? Do we breed and die and that's all? Or is love more? Do we believe that "love never ends"?

18

FAMILY BATHROOM WARS

"There's water all over this bathroom floor. Who was the last one to take a bath – the seal, the polar bear?"

"There's no toothpaste in this tube. What am I supposed to use to brush my teeth – shampoo?"

"Who left the toilet seat up?"

"There's no hot water. I told you we had a small water tank. I have to take a cold shower again?"

"There's no clean towels. In fact, there are no towels. Where are the towels? I'm dripping wet and late for work."

"Hurry up in there. I really have to pee. There's going to be a puddle out here. I swear to God I can't hold it."

SOME MAY THINK these are the bathroom wars that threaten to undo marriages and families. They are not. They are not even battles but mere skirmishes.

The grand battle of all battles, the super war of all super wars, is much more subtle and sinister. It has to do with which way the new roll of toilet paper is installed. Is the loose end closer to the wall or closer to the sitter?

From the male and correct perspective, the roll should hang so the paper goes down next to the wall. It should be positioned in such a way that one pulls up from the back on the hanging loose end. This allows for less friction on the roll, and permits the person sitting to snap off the required number of sheets in such a way that there is indeed a hanging end to grab for the next pull.

From the female and incorrect perspective, the roll is put on so that the loose end is closer to the sitter. The female might think this would be better, but she does not bear in mind one basic law of physics. Once the required number of sheets is separated from the roll, the loose end becomes loose no more. It neatly folds itself close to the roll, so that the end cannot be found.

So, what's the strategy? There are three general approaches to this crisis. Firstly, one can try the-roll spinning technique, placing the fingers squarely upon the top of the roll and pulling in a downward motion in a futile attempt to free the loose end. Secondly, one can take a close look to identify where the loose end actually is. But this is like trying to find the loose end on the scotch tape roll that has nicely adhered to the rest of that roll. The edge or end can only be found by use of a highly powered microscope. The third attack is to use one's fingernails in an upward thrust to somehow get lucky and make contact with the loose end, thus freeing sheets for use. The female approach does not work. Men can see right through all of this. It is simply the incorrect way to install a fresh roll of toilet paper.

This chasm of conflict, this polar opposite view of the universe joins thousands of other impossibilities that exist between man and woman. However, on this occasion, I would like to suggest that this is the most important of all unresolved issues. A lot can be tolerated in relationships. Husbands and wives win and lose battles all the time. But the proper installation of toilet paper on the roll is the issue that can positively lead to separation and eventual divorce. This is where the line is drawn and the cause given.

In divorce court, the woman always relies upon "infidelity" as cause to end marriage. But for the man, it is certainly and invariably "incorrect paper roll replacement!"

19

THUS SPAKE KOHELETH

TWO MEN, ONE age twenty-three, the other age seventy, got into a discussion, of sorts. The twenty-three-year-old began.

"I'm smarter than you."

"You are?"

"Yeah, I'm a lot smarter than you are."

"What makes you think so?"

"I've been to college."

"I went to college."

"Yeah, but you didn't read that much. I've read hundreds of books. That makes me smarter."

"What about life experience? Does that play any part in how smart a person is?"

"Not much. Anything I want to know, I can google or go to Wikipedia. I know how to find out about anything that's out there, anything at all. I am smarter."

The older man inquired, "What does smart mean?"

"It's about intelligence. You old fuddy-duddys don't know anything. You live in the past. The past isn't here anymore. It has little or nothing to do with today and tomorrow."

"So, we just sort of get stupid as we age? Is that it?"

"Well, you surely messed up the world. Look at all the

problems there are. War here. Poverty there. If you had any sense at all, you would have solved some of these problems. But no. You left it all to us in the younger generations to pick up and press on. Of course, we have to be smarter, and we are. Old people just need to face the facts and quit using up valuable air."

"Well, it does seem to be that way. We give ourselves to an occupation our entire lives. We accumulate some knowledge. Then we're told we're overpaid, and they don't need us anymore. They offer us a buy-out into early retirement, and we spend the rest of our days playing shuffleboard on cruises."

The younger man continued, "That's because society knows it doesn't need you anymore. You're like the stud service of a bull. You sire a few and then you're done. You have nothing more to give. Your time on the mountain is over. Move aside and let some of us stronger and younger take over."

"You're sort of contradicting the wisdom of the ages. Society has always revered the wisdom of those who are older. Wise and older men would sit in the coolness in the ancient city gates and serve as judges. People would bring their everyday complaints and conflicts to the old and wise for them to make judgments."

"Yeah, all that stuff was written by old people. Of course, they are going to say that. Listen, old-timer. I don't want to hurt your feelings, but the young have strength, agility, potential, adaptability, creativity, energy, and initiative. Of course, we are going to be more intelligent as well."

"I don't think there's much more I can say then?"

"You got it, old man. Just move out of the way."

"Well, there is one thing," said the old-timer.

"What's that?"

"Get a haircut."

20

MOBY-DICK

AT AGE SEVENTY-TWO, I finished reading *Moby-Dick* by Herman Melville. Of course, the story is known by nearly all, even if they haven't read the book.

Why, in heaven's name, would this book be required English Literature reading for a sixteen-year-old, or a twenty-two-year-old, for that matter? Certainly, at those ages, the brain has developed enough to comprehend the difference between a fo'c's'le and a scuttlebutt, between baleen and spermaceti. But to comprehend the deeper meaning of the story, that is undoubtedly lost on the young.

Herman Melville's vocabulary was immense. His IQ, if it could have been tested back then, would be impressively high. His ability to recall experience was photographic. His research abilities were extensive, especially in an age short on compendia, concordances, and thesauri.

Melville was both educated and brilliant. He knew this about himself. In today's expression, "He was full of himself." Ideas most of us express in five or six words, he chose to use eighty or a hundred. He was a prince of verbiage. Such was the age.

Always, there have been those who near ecstasy reading long strands of carefully chosen and placed words. They quiver at readings. They love words so dearly. They would enjoy every word of Melville's *Moby-Dick*. But there are others of us who prefer the quicker path.

Moby-Dick is a book of fiction, yet with foundation in the true story of the whaling ship *Essex* that was destroyed by a whale. Of course, truth oozes through the pages. The story is simple enough. Captain Ahab loses a leg to a white whale's bite and vows to kill the leviathan. But it is what changes in Ahab's mind and soul that is the lesson. On first glance, it is the injured mortal which is the noble being, and the whale is the sinister beast of ill-will. Read on as the story becomes a matter of twisted justice, of revenge, of obsession.

As the reader looks on from a safe distance, there may be pity felt toward Ahab. He became what we describe today as "damaged goods." Was he embarrassed to lose a fight with a dumb beast? Perhaps he felt emasculated, the ivory peg of a leg the constant reminder that he was less the man he once was.

So, the game is afoot. Melville spins the web. The hunt is not a few weeks' or few months' endeavor. Ahab has spent years searching for his foe. As the days dragged slowly into many years, the hurt deepened, the anger became rage, the fixation of death to Moby-Dick was established as Ahab's sole thought. It all began to eat at his brain, his stomach, his soul. He became a wretch as he brooded. He became a man sick with obsession.

What of Moby-Dick? He was a mammal, swimming his patterns, eating, breeding, actually not a threat except to the smallest of food sources. Moby-Dick had no will. He experienced not the human emotions of revenge, anger, nor the thoughts of strategy and plots.

Sigmund Freud was born five years after the publication of the book. Melville would not have known the word psychology. Yet Melville was a student of human behavior. He weaves the saga of Ahab's slow decline into insanity.

The tars, whalers, and harpooners had heard the rumors flowing concerning the "mental" health of Ahab. But the crew was as salty as he. They knew what could be done with a knife. They could rebel and mutiny if it were called for. They were iron men on wooden ships, strong willed, honed by the exercise of daily chores. What was Ahab but a captain? Yes, due respect, until he goes too far. So, those who didn't think it far enough through signed on to a six-year prison term on the *Pequod*. It might just as well have been prison. There was no escape to freedom aboard a whaling ship. So, the whole crew, with Ishmael spared, became the innocents, the collateral damage when the *Pequod* vortexed into eternal darkness.

The ship was innocent as well. It was not damned or doomed by capricious Olympian gods. It was not cursed or marked or unworthy. The *Pequod* was a ship that got in the way of mindless revenge, of unbridled rage, of a sinister out-of-control obsession.

What of Moby-Dick? Shall we consider him innocent as well? Melville paints him in Ahab's mind as the grand monster of all beasts, but he is simply a mammal, going about his business to survive. What crime? What crime did Moby-Dick commit? Is trying to protect oneself as humans hunt you down with harpoons a crime? What beast from the largest to the smallest does not strike back in a desperate attempt to live?

What is a whale, after all? He's just a mammal, not a human. Ahab twists Moby-Dick into something of his own creation, by personifying, then demonizing. He gives Moby-Dick will and elevates him first to a human, then to that of a devil. But it is Ahab who has will, and as a mortal makes bed with Satan.

What is to be learned from this allegory, this sailor's yarn? Much indeed.

Have we not observed the telltale signs of those who appear to be lambs, but are wolves in disguise?

What are some characteristics of beasts? Beasts are much more than wolves.

Beasts seek to control and do control, stealing human freedom.

Beasts are self-centered and fixated on revenge and getting even.

Beasts are unforgiving and cruel.

Beasts put others at risk and take away their safety.

Beasts withhold the needs of others.

Beast hoard.

Beasts are solitary, unapproachable.

Beasts project their beastly characteristics onto others.

Beasts make those around them less sane.

Beasts often self-destruct.

Have you known beasts? Indeed, they walk among us. What can we do when we encounter a beast? Run. Run! Only the best is strong enough to fight the beast. The rest of us must take flight. Avoid the beast or be led into destruction by the beast.

Children are especially vulnerable. Most parents provide and protect, but the beast is sly, cunning, slippery. Some children are taken in as they are still in process of collecting the data of experience and wisdom. Perhaps they can avoid the beast. Possibly not.

Melville's book shouts loudly, "Beware, beware!" Beware the Ahab beast who walks among you. This is the lesson from *Moby- Dick*. So taught Herman Melville.

21

THROUGH A SON'S YOUNG EYES

Written by Ben Larson-Wolbrink (1996)

"**YOU'RE LUFFING THE** sails." Tearing through the flapping canvas, your Neptune roar jerks me from my daydream of mermaids with soft breasts.

Gripping the tiller with your wood-creased hands, you wrench it from me and pull hard to starboard.

The wind catches the sails again, and we lean into motion as the flapping sail becomes a steadily humming whistle.

"Pull in that jib sheet." Gripping the rope with both hands, I arch my back and lunge backwards, managing to budge the sail inward a few inches before I fumble into the cleat.

You reach over and yank with one arm. The rope is pulled in four feet before you quickly clamp it down.

I see that glint in your eye, chuckling at my puny attempt, or maybe at the wind.

"It's coming out of the south. We'll have a nice down-wind reach heading home." You hand the tiller back to me.

I take it again with a deep breath, and my eyes follow yours to the waves in the distance as they blend into the horizon.

22

EFFECTIVE COURTSHIP

YOUNG PEOPLE TODAY have some strange ways. Just as in all species, males try to attract females, and in some cases, females try to attract males. Peacocks spread their feathers, lions roar, elk butt heads. Animals in the wild seem to be fairly effective at their courtship.

Humans are another matter, and especially humans today. For example, many a young man will start off with this line, apparently thinking it will help him.

"Hey, do you want to do something?" The question is usually rather slurred and uttered with much timidity. The young lady sometimes responds, "Yeah, whatever."

Still others think they're playing their best card with this line. "Want to hang out?" As an older person, I haven't quite figured out what exactly that means. It doesn't seem to convey much enticement or conviction.

The more advanced of the younger male suitors may muster the courage to offer a little more of a specific invitation. "Would you want to go out to dinner and a movie sometime?" Often times that results in a "Yeah," but then he often forgets to get her phone number and they never meet again. Then again, what is it about dinner and a movie? Is that some sort of magic move, assured to net the female in courtship? If I were a woman, it wouldn't do much for me.

I heard a song on the radio the other day. I remember the title, as it was repeated seventy-three times. "I've got my mind set on you." That's nice. But then I heard it over and over again. "I've got my mind set on you. I've got my mind set on you. I've got my mind set on you. I've got my mind set on you. I've got my mind set on you." I don't think endlessly repetitive statements really sway a young lady. I don't think any girl would be convinced of anything more than that the chap has a pretty small vocabulary.

Oh my God. Can't you come up with a second line? Convince me. Persuade me. Lure me. Beating me to death with the same old line doesn't do much at all.

Young people are so inept, one wonders if the human species will survive. It probably will, with so much sex being had by everybody. As I understand it, there really doesn't need to be much of a display of feathers today at all, not much of a courtship dance. In lieu of these traditional maneuvers, it's straight to the motel for heavy breathing. Then, they say something fairly obvious: "Man, that was great." Really?

Of course, it's great. Were it not great, we'd make no effort at all to procreate. It's like young people are surprised to discover that when parts are put together, they generally work well. It's a simple enough act. But having sex today has little or nothing to do with courtship. Dogs can do it in the alley. Funniest tee-shirt I ever saw: "I can do it." Really. Is that all you can do? Pill bugs and elephants can "do it." If that's all you're bragging about, you have very little to boast.

Superbowl half-time shows look like orgies. Concerts with folks barely dressed have little to do with music. Has anybody ever reflected that it seems the more we expose of our bodies, the less the intimate act of sex seems to mean? Perhaps, this is a slight tangent from the issue at hand.

There was once this wonderful phrase used by us "old

folks." Lots of people used it and understood it. Men used to put tons of energy, time, effort, prayer, money into "winning the heart of a lady." Today, there would be those who would say that this phrase is not politically correct. Whatever.

Can we remember the dignity and respect in that concept? – "winning the heart of a lady?" This is not making a woman an idol or a deity. This is just simple kindness, respect, appreciation.

I knew a couple who spent their whole lives together, happily married to the very end. This is their story. When Robert Nilsson met Nellie Lindberg, they were both just entering 9th grade. Their desks were near and they smiled to one another.

After class, Bob asked Nellie about her thoughts on the English assignment they had. Then, Nellie asked Bob if he could help her with some mathematics. They had lunch together and talked some more.

Bob made a decision about Nellie, but he would keep that decision to himself for four years. During those four years, Nellie and Bob would walk home from school together, go roller skating, visit each other's families at holiday times. They got in snowball fights with the other kids and would go down to the swimming hole in the summertime.

But when Bob wasn't at school, doing homework or chores, or otherwise involved, he was in the home basement working on a project. His father helped him make a drawing of the idea, and Bob was free to use all his father's tools. But the project involved wood, expensive wood, so Bob had to get a job at the hardware store and saved some money.

He picked red mahogany, a strong hardwood, and finally bought enough to get started. He turned legs on the lathe and hand carved lion claw legs. He made drawers, twenty-one of them, three rows of seven, with tongue and groove joints. He bought mirrors and cut the glass. Hinges, chains, handles, knobs were all needed. Bob was building something pretty special, something pretty big. In fact, when it was finished, it stood five feet tall, was twenty-four inches wide, and a foot deep. He stained the mahogany with red mahogany stain, then applied five coats of varnish. The drawers were softened with felt and velvet. Two big doors enclosed the structure, and he installed a lock and key.

Bob spent countless hours over a period of four years and never said a word to Nellie. He was making this gift for Nellie and would present it to her upon the occasion of their high school graduation. It was a jewelry cabinet, and a significant one at that.

Bob and Nellie continued in their relationship, in the ups and downs, and ebbs and flows of getting to know each other. Bob's mind hadn't changed a bit from that decision day in 9th grade. He knew exactly what he was doing. He never fell off the path from his purpose.

He built this beautiful, one of a kind, handmade jewelry cabinet to give to Nellie. His purpose was simple. He intended to win the lady's heart, and, of course, he did.

The surprise in Nellie's eyes when he unveiled her own handmade jewelry cabinet! She ran and threw her arms around Bob's neck. They smiled together. He had won her heart.

Men, if it is among your aims in life to win a woman's heart, there are some futile ways and some fruitful ways to do it. Winning a woman's heart is not so simple as choosing between chicken and hamburger at the restaurant. This is something BIG, men, something really BIG. Do it right. Don't be a jerk. Be a Bob Nilsson. Win a woman's heart, and she will love you forever.

23

SELF-AWARENESS

IT HAS BEEN said, "We are three people: who others think we are, who we think we are, and who God thinks we are." The last, who God thinks we are, is such a vast topic, we'll hop over it and on to the idea who others think we are.

Others may think us idiots or brilliant. Others may think we're kind or ruthless. Others may think we're introverted or extroverted. Others may think we're Republicans or Democrats. Others may think we are exciting to be around or boring. Few will really tell you what they think about you. Consider any two of your friends. They each may have polar opposite views or who you are. Primarily, that is because they have only had partial and limited experience of you. Thus, all their opinions are prejudiced, incomplete.

This being said, there are many who care a great deal about what others think about them. Therefore, they dress to be approved and liked. They do things they think others like to do. They are people- pleasers. They define themselves by the standard of what others might think about them. I think this is the most slippery of all slippery slopes. Public opinion is as reliable as the restless seas, changing at every moment. We change our minds about what we think about certain individuals all the time. Why would we give that much of our concern to what others might think about us?

Shakespeare wrote of Polonius' advice to Laertes, "To thine own-self be true, and it must follow, as the night the day, thou canst not then be false to any man." So, now begins the Herculean task, that of being true to oneself. And in order to be true to oneself, one must know oneself. Do you know who you are? What do you think about yourself? The task of self-awareness is a lifelong endeavor.

Sigmund Freud advanced the idea of introspection. It was an every-night process for him. As he ended each day, he would block out time to reflect upon his own conscious thoughts and feelings. He named this process introspection. He would review in his mind conversations, reactions, words spoken, actions taken. He would replay the day in his mind order to arrive at a deeper insight concerning who he was.

Self-awareness requires that we ask questions of ourselves over and over again.

> Why did I say that?
>
> Why did I do that?
>
> Was I in conversation, sharing thoughts and feelings, or was I defending myself?
>
> Was I unpleasant to the other? Why? Did I gain something by so doing?
>
> Did somebody say or do something that upset me? Why did it upset me?
>
> Was somebody kind to me? Why were they kind to me?
>
> Do I find myself falling into old patterns of conversation which really don't engage the other person? Why?
>
> Am I defensive? Do I need to be? Was I under attack?

If I find myself having certain feelings, are those the feelings I want to have?

How can I change thoughts and feelings I don't particularly like?

Can I change? Why should I change? How can I change?

Am I taking responsibility for my thoughts and feelings or am I blaming others or circumstances that I feel the way I do?

How much of my life is involved with escape? Are my escapes healthy?

How much of my life am I protecting myself? Do I need to build high walls around myself for protection?

Are others out to get me?

Has anything good occurred today?

Were any of my worst fears actualized?

Am I becoming more of who I want to become?

Am I in a rut with certain relationships? What can I do to move forward?

Am I running away from myself? Am I afraid of my thoughts and feelings?

Why do I become angry? Why do I cry?

What makes me want to give up and think the worst about people?

What makes me joyful about other people?

What give me hope?

What dashes my hope?

Why am I anxious? Do I need to be anxious?

Am I safe or not safe?

Did I do anything to help anything or anybody today?

Did I have a positive impact or a negative impact on today? Why would I want to do either?

Am I dealing with my self-awareness in a helpful, progressive manner or do I need to seek the help of others who could be sounding boards, guides, who could help me see new perspectives?

The questions above are just a small sampling of the many reflections that might occur with introspection, along the journey of self-awareness. These questions are just the beginning points, primes for the water pump, knowing that there are thousands more good questions to consider, good reflections to ponder.

Dealing with the question "Who am I?" is not for the faint of heart. It is nothing less than a mountaintop and deep valley experience. Everyone who reflects about who he/she is will experience profound joys and profound sadness.

Self-awareness. Who do I think I am, as a man, in general, in this situation or that, or in this very second of life?

Many don't bother taking this road. They're on a bypass and want nothing to do with such notions. I've heard so many say, "I have no idea who I am." That's a sad statement. One might just as well be dead, then. If one has no idea who they are, then they are nothing. I don't mean to be rude here, but that's the logical conclusion. One might just as well be a cat, or an acorn, or dead. Self-awareness is part of human life. It's part of our marching orders. Get busy and spend your whole life engaged in the process. Otherwise, tell me why are you using up precious air and water.

Confucius offered the following proverb.

He who knows not, knows not, he knows not is a fool, shun him.

He who knows not and he knows not, he is simple, teach him.

He who knows and knows not that he knows, he is asleep, wake him.

He who knows and knows that he knows is wise, follow him.

This is not a new idea. Socrates uttered the words long ago: "The unexamined life is not worth living." (470 – 399 BCE)

24

HISTORY, MYSTERY, AND THE PRESENT

"**THE PAST IS** history. The future is mystery. The present is a present." This is a powerful juxtaposition of three thoughts which considered together require some reflection.

The past is history. It may be assumed that history is some sort of static, unchangeable entity. Many think so. But, in fact, history is continually re-examined and analyzed. It takes on new information, new meanings. History ebbs, flows, evolves. History is somewhat cyclical and repeats itself, at least in terms of trends and cycles. Some argue that history is only cyclical. Others argue that history is lineal, traveling along some straight path from beginning to end. I have chosen to consider that history is spiral, that is, both cyclical and lineal. It's rather like a "Slinky" toy stretched out. It does have a forward (or backwards) movement, yet repeats the larger issues. So, exactly what is it that we receive, when we receive history?

The future is mystery. Yes, to some degree the future is all educated guesswork, and often wrong by the "predictors" who tell us how the future will be. The stock market thrives on futures, the guesswork concerning which stocks will grow and by how much. Tomorrow is unknown. Who knows what will happen? Yet the odds are extremely high that the sun will rise again, or more properly, that the earth will turn. Odds are that we'll have enough air and food to continue our task of survival. Tomorrow will be much like today and maybe not so much a mystery.

The present is the present. Ah, a play on words and ideas. Today is a gift, in other words, as if the past and the future were not gifts. Why are they not gifts as well? Perhaps it is insinuated that we only have this moment in which to really live, this millisecond of life. I continue to compose in the expectation that I might complete this book, that I probably will, that I will have many tomorrows which will be as much a gift as today is.

"Be alive in the present moment," we are exhorted by those who think others are not doing it properly. "Don't live in the past – it's over the gone. The future? "Que sera, sera, whatever will be, will be." Just focus on the present moment – that's the gift."

In this present moment I'm having a root canal. I don't want to live in this present moment. Indeed, I am imaging a much happier future, after the root canal, when my jaw won't be stretched out and my gums and teeth not sore. I don't like this present moment. If it's a gift, where's the exchange booth?

This time machine marches on. But in our minds, we are in many times at the same time. We remember experiences. We imagine the future. We do the present, but we move so freely along the time chart that we're not aware we are doing it.

We're mostly sure that death will end our time, at least our time here. We know our bodies will decompose (over time), and earth return to earth, and dust return to dust. A great percentage of our population believes in reincarnation, and still others believe in resurrection. Both beliefs assert that there will be more time after time ends. If somebody tells you that they "know" these things, run like hell. They don't know. No matter how loudly they sing, "I know that my Redeemer liveth," they really don't know. The truth is we are all agnostics – we simply can't know. I ate that fish. His time is over. He's a goner. Period. He, or she, doesn't get any more past, present, or future.

Then, there's the recycle argument. Our chemicals go into other living things, so we live on. We have dinosaurs and stardust in us, and termites, green beans, oak trees, sharks...yeah, yeah. I can take comfort in that? Right.

Do time's feelings get hurt when we don't use it rightly? When we ignore time, forget time, abuse time, waste time, does time pout? Is somebody making a log of our use of time? Good time, bad time, useful time, wasted time. Who's to know? Who's to judge? If God, or St. Peter, meets us at the pearly gates and does a review of our time, it's going to take an awfully long time. There'll be a lot of people waiting in that line. "Hurry on, up there. My cloud's leaving the station soon." St. Peter's adding machine is just humming. Good time. Bad time. Times of grace. Times of sinning. Here's the total. Oh, I'm sorry, you are just ten good seconds shy on the good side of the ledger, so down you go. Enjoy hell and say hello to the others down there.

25

WORDS WE LIVE BY

IT USED TO be that we lived by words. Two generations before us, when students graduated from high school, each had a command and understanding of approximately 25,000 words. Today, the average (United States) high school graduate commands approximately 5,000 words, or if fairly studious, maybe 10,000 words. Not only has the extent of our vocabulary diminished, but our understanding as well. When the "F" word is used three times in every broken sentence, it means just about anything we may want it to mean.

Years ago, we heard the common expression, "My word is my bond." One's word was better than a written contract. It carried with it one's reputation, one's honesty and integrity, one's reliability, one's trustworthiness. "You have my word," meant that you can count on me. I will not only "talk the talk, but walk the walk."

In the ancient Hebrews' language of the Old Testament, the word in Hebrew "dabar," literally meant "word/deed." The word for word was the same as the word for deed. When something was spoken, it happened. When God spoke, the world was created. The action followed the word, or in essence occurred at the same time. Thus, words were carefully selected and used (up until the last fifty years or so). One would not curse another human, as that curse would necessarily result in that curse happening. We believed that words were that powerful.

When the Old Testament prophet Amos went into the northern kingdom to deliver a dark and stark message to the evil king, it is written that "the land was not able to bear up under the weight of his words." Words used to be powerful.

Anyone who reads a classic novel today cannot but be impressed by the language used. Colorful, descriptive words were sewn together into a tapestry of expression that could make us stop in our tracks. Book words were so profoundly elegant.

Now, we're little more than a pack of liars. We say one thing here and another thing there. We are so "relative" and "situational" that words are no longer the bastions and foundations of our living. Smart attorneys, who still know words, can persuade a jury to believe black is white and white is black.

Here's the secret, if it has not already been known or discovered by the reader. The "word is [still] mightier than the sword," whether or not we know it or live it. Words rule.

So that we do not limit our understanding here, I mean words in the broadest of understandings. Languages are words. Many leaders of today's world are multi-lingual, as we Americans dig in and demand that only English be spoken. Is it any wonder we are so far behind?

Mathematics is words. Computers are words. Science is words. Money is words. Politics is words. Energy is words. It was when Helen Keller discovered words that she was reborn, that her universe was opened and she was alive for the first time. Anne Sullivan worked and worked with blind and deaf Helen until the breakthrough. Keller later wrote in her autobiography,

> As the cool stream gushed over one hand she spelled into the other the word water, first slowly, then rapidly.

I stood still, my whole attention fixed upon the motions of her fingers. Suddenly I felt a misty consciousness as of something forgotten – a thrill of returning thought; and somehow the mystery of language was revealed to me. I knew then that "w-a-t-e-r" meant the wonderful cool something that was flowing over my hand. That living word awakened my soul, gave it light, hope, joy, set it free! There were barriers still, it is true, but barriers that could in time be swept away.

Words give us light, hope, joy, and set us free.

People live without reflection, without thinking over their words and actions. They just do. They respond to stimuli without much thought. But I believe above all that we live by words. Some people know their words. Many do not. There are words out there, powerful words that have served as beacon lights to guide generations along life's way.

The ancient Jews lived by the words of the Torah and especially the Ten Commandments. "I am the Lord, Thy God. You shall have no other Gods before me." Christians live by the summary Jesus gave, "As you would that men would do unto you, do so unto them." Every faith religion has words it lives by.

The Hippocratic Oath was written in the 5th century BC to uphold the art of medicine. "Do no harm." Clubs and organizations have words they live by: Masons, Elks, Lions, Rotary, etc.

Scouting has words they live by. The Scout motto written in 1907, "Be Prepared." And the Scout Oath.

On my honor, I will do my best, to do my duty to God and my country, and to obey the Scout law; to help other people at all times, to keep myself physically strong, mentally awake, and morally straight.

I had a good friend who was so taken by Charles Dickens' words that he kept copy in his wallet and took it with him wherever he went.

> Whatever I have tried to do in life, I have tried with all my heart to do it well, whatever I have devoted myself to, I have devoted myself completely, in great aims and in small I have always thoroughly been in earnest.

There is no end to the credos, creeds, declarations, ideals that have been created over the course of human history to guide us. There is no end to the many principles, laws, proverbs that inspire us to live better. Thanks to Google and Wikipedia, the reader may explore any number of resources. If you're not familiar, check out "Desiderata" written by Max Ehrmann (1872-1945).

What are my words? What words do I live by? Upon my high school graduation, I was given a congratulations card with a writing by Rudyard Kipling, entitled "If." It has become a big part of my guiding light through life. It is worth the read.

> If you can keep your head, when all about you are losing theirs, and blaming it on you.

> If you can trust yourself when all men doubt you, but make allowance for their doubting too.

> If you can wait, but not be tired by waiting, or being lied about, don't deal in lies, or being hatred, don't give way to hating. And yet, don't look too good, nor talk too wise.

> If you can dream and not make dreams your master.

> If you can think and not make thoughts your aim.

If you can meet with triumph and disaster, and treat those two imposters just the same.

If you can bear to hear the truth you've spoken, twisted by knaves to make a trap for fools, or watch the things you gave your life to, broken, and stoop and build 'em up with worn out tools.

If you can make one heap of all your winnings and risk it on one turn of pitch-and-toss, and lose, and start again at your beginnings, and never breathe a word about your loss.

If you can force your heart and nerve and sinew to serve your turn long after they are gone, and so hold on when there is nothing in you except the will which says to them, "hold on."

If you can walk with crowds and keep your virtue, or walk with kings – nor lose the common touch.

If neither foes nor loving friends can hurt you. If all men count with you, but none too much.

If you can fill the unforgiving minute with 60 seconds worth of distance run –yours is the Earth and everything that's in it, and – which is more- you'll be a Man, my son.

How many times I have pulled out these words and read them, again and again. They remind me of the things that are important, of the behaviors I want to live. And let's not slip into the fatalism that says that the "real" will never achieve the "ideal." I'm not ready to stop trying.

Abraham Lincoln faced an impossible task. A mother in the north had lost all five of her sons in battles fighting for the preservation of the Union. He attempted a response. These are the words of a letter he sent.

> Executive Mansion
> Washington, D.C. Nov. 21, 1864
>
> To Mrs. Bixby, Boston, Mass,
>
> Dear Madam,
> I have been shown in the files of the War Department a statement of the adjutant General of Massachusetts that you are the mother of five sons who have died gloriously in the field of battle. I feel how weak and fruitless must be any word of mine which should attempt to beguile you from the grief of a loss so overwhelming. But I cannot refrain from tendering you the consolation that may be found in the thanks of the republic they died to save. I pray that our heavenly father may assuage the anguish of your bereavement, and leave you only the cherished memory of the loved and lost, and the solemn pride that must be yours to have laid so costly a sacrifice upon the altar of freedom.
>
> > Yours very sincerely and respectfully,
> > Lincoln

Nothing could take away that mother's horrific pain. Yet, Lincoln used the very best words he had at his command to address the issue and help in a way he felt he needed to help. Words we live by.

Perhaps you are considering for yourselves the question, "What are the words that you, the reader, live by?" Personalize this otherwise third person discussion. What are the words you live by? Each of us has his or her own credo. It would be well to take some time and consider the questions?

- What words guide my life?
- What words stand as lighthouses in my stormy sea?

- What words are the ground of my being, upon which I stand?
- What words would I want other to say about me?
- What words might be a summary of my unique life?

It's a valuable exercise, I think. It's important for each of us to know what we know, and to be able to say in words why we do what we do.

To continue this discussion, I've spent many hours myself, trying to identify and clarify the words that I live by. I engaged in this exercise decades ago, and each time I revisit my words, I find that they are still my words. They are my words. It doesn't matter if others agree with MY words. And your words should be unique for you.

In brief summary, I have four words. Perhaps they may seem like curious words, standing on their own, but I'd like to amplify with some brief explanation of how I understand each of my words. They are:

Balance

Tolerance

Perspective

Community

Firstly, what is balance? A very influential book in my life, written by Parker Palmer was entitled *The Promise of Paradox*. Among his insights is that life seems to be about opposites: black and white, rich and poor, up and down, healthy and sick, alive and dead, happy and sad. These words/ideas are opposites along a continuum. Palmer does a stellar job of exploring the question, "What do we do about this?" For me it is about balance. There is no way to escape the low or negative sides of the continuum, any more that we can move to the positive side and always stay there. Said simply, we cannot avoid being sometimes sad, and we can't always be happy. So, my trick is to find balance and to understand that both ends on the continuum are present in my life and, in fact, needed.

Remember how we balanced out the teeter-totter? One large kid on one end and two skinny kids on the other. Or some teeter-totters even came equipped such that the board could be slid closer to one side. Ah, physics at play.

Sleep hours are usually around eight. Awake times are usually around sixteen. When I keep that in balance, things seem to go pretty well. Too much being awake, too little sleep, not so good.

One of my theories about living in the northeast of the United States is that the seasons are all wrong. The way it is set up, and I don't know who to blame here, there are approximately three months of each of the four seasons. But three months of winter is too long. We get sick and tired of three months of winter. One-and-one-half months of winter would be better. Three months of summer is too long also. Yeah, we all live for summer, but about the time hot August comes around and the mosquitoes and flies are at their peak, we're ready for a change. Summer would be better if it were only one-and-one-half months long. The seasons are out of balance. Spring and fall are just the same. Too much of the same thing. We're ready to move on.

I don't know where the complaint department is on this one, but I hope to submit a letter someday that suggests that we go through the four seasons twice in every year. A month and a half of winter, then we move onto a month and a half of spring, and so on. Wouldn't things be in better balance if it went that way? Who can I complain to? I'd like to get this in better balance.

Second, is tolerance. We need to see the larger meaning of the word. It means much more than simply, "I can tolerate (put up with) this, that, or whatever." Tolerance has to do with elasticity. It has to do with an entity being able to stretch and not break. A rubber band is good only if it continues to stretch and be elastic. If it breaks, a rubber band is simply no good.

Tolerance can be taught. Tolerance can increase. Yoga is all about stretching the joints, making our bodies elastic again. Aging is an awful journey toward IN-tolerance. We become stiff and rigid, and given enough stress, we break. If we remain tolerant, we bend with the pressures.

The old oak tree grew plenty tall. It had been around for years and years. Its trunk was big enough for a human to hide behind. Its branches could hold the nests of dozens of squirrels and birds. Its leaves were abundant and gave shade to many. The old oak tree was strong, straight until the hurricane winds came to call. Then the old oak tree broke in two and fell to its death. But there stood the young sapling whose trunk was only a couple inches in diameter. There stood the sapling who only rose into the sky, a mere fifteen feet tall. The sapling stood because it was tolerant, elastic, and bent with the force of the hurricane winds. It survived.

There is an aging force in life which fights against our tolerance, and we must fight back. If we become rigid in body, we will break. If we become rigid in mind and spirit, we will break. If we take our ideas and thoughts and chisel them into stone, they will crumble in time. Only, if we are tolerant can we continue on.

The third word I live by is perspective. There is an old proverb that goes, "One can't see the forest for the trees." Indeed, when we are traipsing around in the forest, we can only see the trees. We can't see the entire forest for what it is. Another saying goes, "When one is up to one's waist in alligators, it's hard to remember that the purpose was to drain the swamp." Both proverbs seem to suggest that when we're too close to a situation, we may not be able to see the situation for what it is.

What glory it is to look out an airplane window and see the fields, towns, buildings, night lights below. What glory it was for the astronauts to look out and see our little earth as a blue/green ball floating in space. What perspective that gave.

We need perspective to contend with our daily issues. We need to look at life from the long view as well as close up. As a sailor, I have been caught in many storms. I think it may be one of the scariest experiences a person can have. It's hard to share what it is like to see lightning bolts at night, thunder that rumbles your vessel, waves so high that water cascades into one's boat, wind that can blow your clothes off. I have told myself many times, "This will end," because when I've been in the midst of that awful time, I think it won't end. But it does. Remembering perspective gets us through some of the stormy seas of life.

When we are ill, we lose perspective. Who among us, when we have been very ill, has not had the thought, "Was I ever healthy? Will I ever be healthy again?" But with perspective, we know that we will most likely be healthy again.

I believe every person tries to do the best he or she can do in life. But many of us, in our work lives have to make hard decisions that are more grey than black and white. Sometimes I have had to tell myself that 51% is better than 49%, but I know that it might have just as easily gone the other way. This has resulted in sleepless nights, and some frettin' and fussin'. Until I tell myself, "One hundred years from now, what will it matter?" That's perspective. Regaining perspective has saved me many times.

Comedian George Carlin died in 2008. One might not think a comedian could write such an eloquent observation of perspective, but that he did. These are his words.

> The paradox of our time in history is that we have taller buildings, but shorter tempers, wider Freeways, but narrower viewpoints. We spend more, but have less; we buy more, but enjoy less. We have bigger houses and smaller families, more conveniences, but less time.

We have more degrees but less sense, more knowledge, but less judgement, more experts, yet more problems, more medicine, but less wellness. We drink too much, smoke too much, spend too recklessly, laugh too little, drive too fast, get too angry, stay up too late, get up too tired, watch TV too much, and pray too seldom. We have multiplied our possessions, but reduced our values. We talk too much, love too seldom, and hate too often. We've learned how to make a living, but not a life. We've added years to life but not life to years.... We've cleaned up the air, but polluted the soul. We've conquered the atom, but not our prejudice....These are the times of fast foods and slow digestion, big men and small characters, steep profits and shallow relationships. These are the days of two incomes but more divorce, fancier houses, but broken homes.

That is called "getting perspective."
The fourth word I try to live by and always have in mind is community. We are born into community. There's mother and father, then along comes me, making three. We are by design meant to be in community. Probably, instantly, we are a part of a tribe or clan. There are grandparents, uncles and aunts, cousins.

Then begins a whole series of other communities: church and Sunday school, preschool, school, scouts, choirs, athletic teams, colleges, work places, etc.

John Donne (1624) wrote:

"No man is an island, entire of it-self, every man a piece of the Continent, a part of the main."

The Apostle Paul picked up on the same theme in I Corinthians 12,

The eye cannot say to the hand, "I don't need you." And the hand cannot say to the feet, "I don't need you." So that there should be no division in the body, but that its parts should have equal concern for each other."

The quotes are endless. Abraham Lincoln said, "A nation divided against itself cannot stand."

True there are those who argue the case for the individual. Frank Sinatra bellowed out, "I did it my way." Rugged American Individualism, did indeed, settle America. But there would be no "I" without "we," no "me" without "they."

In this modern age, most are beginning to see how truly interdependent we are to each other. No nation can make it alone anymore. By trade, travel, sports, leisure, we are tied to each other as never before. As many have said, when one falls, we all fall. When one succeeds, we all succeed.

Ecosystems tie us together into one world community. A nuclear disaster in Chernobyl affects us here. A tsunami in Indonesia affects us here. A stock market blip in the US affects the whole world. We all must be aware that 90% of American medical tests are done somewhere else than in the US. There is no "them" and "us" anymore. We make it as one world community, or we will not make it.

Of course, not all believe this. There' s a panic, and the supermarket shelves are empty of toilet paper and paper products. If anybody can explain this phenomenon, I would surely like to understand. Certainly, at the base of it all is selfishness.

When things go well, we might persuade ourselves that we don't need "those others." But when things are not good, how we run to those who can help. Community is our survival.

26

DISTRACTION

IT WAS LIKELY during the darkest hour of night, or on another black occasion, that the Great Confuser snuck by and attached an iron ball and chain to your leg. The ball is symbolic of your particular crushing pain, each individual ball designed for each unique person

The world's pains are numerous. A loved one's death, a financial loss, dashed hope, lost job or disappointment, a suffering of some sort. It does not significantly matter how it came to you or when it came to you. But, from a certain moment in the sojourn of your life, the ball and chain were attached. They will be there until your death.

Removal is not an option. Understandably, we attempt to ignore it, to somehow pretend that it is not there. However, shackles, balls and chains, being what they are, they make it difficult to ignore...and to get around. They are heavy, noisy. The sharp, cold metal cuts into the leg. They are a constant companion and reminder.

Paradox, being what life is, we stand between pain and distraction. Some lose the struggle of paradox. They live with pain all the time and are rarely, if ever, distracted. Others are able to distract to varying degrees.

We fill our lives with other preoccupations, other thoughts, other obligations. Our calendars are full of distractions that momentarily neutralize the pain. We drug ourselves, literally or symbolically, so we can carry on bravely and pretend to others that we have no ball and chain. "We're doing just fine." We lie to ourselves and others.

Perhaps, distraction is a balm in Gilead. Perhaps distraction is grace, a gift of coping, a power to receive. Perhaps we've been looking at the coin wrong side up?

Did not a benevolent power come to us on the brighter of days with laughter and love? We have all laughed and loved once or more. We may have laughed and loved many times. Do we forget this? Further, why do we doubt that they are the stronger force?

Pain steals in, yet there are loved ones near, close enough to feel, near enough to touch. We receive their prayers, hopes, well-wishes, sympathy, and understanding. Does not what we receive from them give us strength?

No one can deny life's great pains, the cruel and awful pains. They are there like a ball and chain. Yet, too, in our bondage, we oft see the light of day, the loving hand, the kindred spirit. Grace and charity do come to all. If love is simply a distraction, then it is the most powerful of all gifts to life.

27

GRANDMA'S BIG LIE

AT A FIFTIETH wedding anniversary gathering, Grandma was asked what the success of her long marriage was. She smiled and said, "Well, we never argued, not once. We just didn't do it. Every day of our life together there has been harmony. I suppose you could say, we've been in love for fifty years. Longer. When folks are in love, they don't fight, argue or disagree."

The interviewer immediately turned his attention to Grandpa, sitting over to the side, fiddling with his pipe and tobacco. "Would you agree with what Grandma said?"

"Say what?" he responded.

Shouting as loud as the inquirer could, he asked, "GRAMMA SAYS YOU NEVER FOUGHT OR ARGUED."

"Say what?" Grandpa answered again. "Don't you know I can't hear? I'm stone deaf; been so for years."

Ah, so that's it. You and Grandpa never argued because Grandpa couldn't hear a word you had to say. He just turned a deaf ear and smiled all these years, and you interpreted that as marital harmony. Come on, Grandma. Come on. You never argued? Arguing has been a part of the marriage covenant since the beginning.

We all remember that conversation between Adam and Eve.

"Why did you tempt me to eat that apple?"

"I did not tempt you to do anything?"

"Yes, you did. You tempted me."

"I don't have any idea what you're talking about."

"Yes, you do. Yes, you do. Who was it came slinking by here, swiveling her hips this way and that? Who was it said, 'Want a bite, big boy?' That's you who said that."

"I did not slink by here, you horny jerk. All you do is sit around here, drinking beer all day and watching the garden grow. Why don't you go out and get a job, you worthless bum."

That's just how the conversation was recorded in the first book of the scriptures – "Genitals."

Husbands and wives have been arguing ever since. There's not been a marriage, ever, where the husband and wife didn't fight.

Of course, years ago, the clergy left off that part in the marriage ceremony, but everybody knew it used to be there. Just after "in sickness and in health" was the question "Will you argue just about every day?" That used to be in the wedding ceremony. Now, it's all implied. It's a given in all marriages. It's so well understood, it doesn't have to be said anymore.

They say "Denial is not a river in Egypt." Why do we deny so, and pretend that we're this way and not that way? Who are you trying to impress, Grandma, you who never argued once in all your married days? Are you trying to put on a good front for the grandkids? How can what you say be believed?

Oh, there are the sweet ones out there. They see only lemonade when given lemons. They see only opportunity when faced with tragedy. If it's a dark, stormy, rainy day, the sun has got to be shining somewhere. They know the song so well, "When you're smiling, the whole world smiles with you."

I applaud the effort. I really do. Bliss is a choice, to a certain degree, as misery is sometimes. "Stiff upper lip, eh what?" the Brits say to each other. They also have that wonderful saying, "Keep your pecker up," and that doesn't mean what you think it means, you naughty boy.

Look at that face on Grandma. Of course, she's happy. The evidence is there. Fifty years. It must have been something. After all, arguing causes stress, and stress closes down the blood flow, and voilà, you're dead. So, be happy, even when maybe you're not.

I suppose it all has to do with how one argues. A great many people have not learned the fine art. Someone says, "Man, you're ugly." The other one pulls out a gun and shoots him. Bam. Dead. A lifetime in prison just because he never learned how to argue.

Don't they teach it anymore? It should be a gentle thing at first. One doesn't turn to the "triple dog dare" without the former steps being taken first. Where's the courtesy anymore? "I say, ol' chap, I have to take issue with that last point of yours. I just don't quite see it that way. I'd like to suggest that you consider...." That's how it should go. No need to reach for the gun when the gate is dropped and the race has just begun. Were others in other times and places so testy? It sometimes seems like everybody is walking around at 211 degrees, just a smidgeon below the boiling point. Anybody know where the switch is on the stove? I'd like to turn it down. Maybe that's all Grandma was trying to do—turn down the heat. Add some experience to this volatile moment in which we live. Grandma might be asking, "What's the fuss?" Is it worth it all this stress and tension and ill will?

"Let peace on earth begin, and let it begin with me." Some of us just throw up when we hear that song. How can we not argue against injustice, against inequality, against poverty, against war? How can we not protest and march? How can we not have righteousness indignation over the plight of those who have not been heard, cannot be heard over the laughter of the Daddy Warbucks of the earth?

I've tried to be more like Grandma. I really have. I loved her so. She is so right. Why argue? The Peace Train is the way to go. But I just can't do it. I can't see how this will help. Will

Grandma's smiling face turn off the ovens at Auschwitz? No. there must be those who argue, those who face off, eyeball to eyeball with the devils and demons, those who ruin this good thing called life.

It's Mother Theresa who is credited with the following writing, although there have been additions and deletions. The next thoughts were from a saint.

> People are illogical, unreasonable, and self-centered. Love them anyway.
>
> If you do good, people will accuse you of selfish, ulterior motives. Do good anyway.
>
> If you are successful, you will make false friends and true enemies. Succeed anyway.
>
> The good you do today will be forgotten tomorrow. Do good anyway.
>
> Honesty and frankness make you vulnerable. Be honest and frank anyway.
>
> The biggest man with the biggest ideas can be shot down by the smallest men with the smallest minds. Think big anyway.
>
> People favor underdogs but follow only top dogs. Fight for underdogs anyway.
>
> What you spend years building up may be destroyed overnight. Build anyway.
>
> People really need help, but they may attack you if you do help them. Help them anyway.
>
> Give the world the best you have and you'll get kicked in the teeth. Give the world the best you have anyway.

Have you ever heard more difficult words? Oh, they're sweet to read. Sign me up, for sure. Then there's the application, the living out of the ideals, making reality out of lofty principles.

How many times can New Year's Resolutions be broken before we just stop trying? Failure after failure.

The Apostle Paul said, "Why is it the good I would do, I don't do, and that which I would not do, I do?" Is the mind willing and the flesh weak?

I see-saw back and forth. Decisions become more difficult to make. The correct ethic, the real truth, the most helpful thing to say or do. All have become more elusive.

Grandma. Grandma. I miss you so. I need to hear your wisdom again.

28

THE COMMON SENSE OF MODERATION

PERHAPS THE EARLIEST use of the concept of moderation comes from the ancient Greek historian Hesiod, who said, "moderation is best in all things." Euripides echoed the concept as did many more, including Aristotle.

The opposite of moderation would be extremism. Why would moderation be desirable and extremism not so? It's not such a simple question.

In today's news circles, it's extremism that sells papers and goes viral, not moderation. We have heard so much inflammatory language we are desensitized to it: catastrophe, disaster, crisis, Armageddon, panic, fear, total breakdown. None of these apply to today's news stories, but these emotionally inflated words have to be used to get people to watch. A station that airs a ten-year-old going into a school with a gun requires that all others be on the look-out for a nine-year old with a gun. We seem to be excited about the extreme. It's a thrill.

In the gym is heard the exhortation for "extreme training and fitness." If there's no pain, there's no gain. Jogging a few miles is not good enough anymore. We have to do the Iron

Man marathon. Hiking a hill has been replaced by scaling the sheer face of a mountain with ropes and pitons.

Drinking is no longer a pint at the pub but binge drinking, getting wasted, passing out. We binge eat called gorging. America's weight problem is a problem indeed. We binge watch television. We "get into" series that last sixty episodes, ninety episodes. Bingeing is extreme behavior.

Hoarding is extremism. Never have we had such an abundance of goods, and many fill their homes with everything, from food to toilet paper, to old magazines and stuff that can't be thrown out. Many a home has stacks of cartons, more clothes in the closet that one could ever wear, broken toys, jars, cans. Hoarding is the extreme end of consumerism.

Tattoos are a curiosity. They began with sailors wanting to remember island girls they met on their voyages. Now everyone has a "tat." They do have a wonderful purpose, especially on women who have had mastectomies or others who have had their bodies damaged in a myriad of ways. Tattoos become a statement of positivity, "I am still beautiful." However, the most bizarre email I ever received was entitled, "Mommy, why can't I get a job?" There followed about thirty photographs of people whose God-given skin was gone. Tattoos covered them all from head to toe. And then there were metal, rings, rods, stuck through every conceivable part of the body. Intentional scarring and cutting were apparent. Is this moderate tattooing or extremism?

Before we approach some thoughts on moderation, let's return to this chapter's title words, "Common Sense." Thomas Paine borrowed this phrase for his 1775 pamphlets advocating independence from Great Britain. The idea of "common sense" became common thereafter. But the idea is not so common today.

There was a time when our living was more common. We were all on the farm. We all milked cows, sowed corn, repaired tractors, went to church, etc. We had common experience from which to learn common sense. Some did have the sense to learn from their experience; others did not. Today, our living has become so individualistic in America that there is little left common among us. Instead of heading down to the grange, we drive to hockey practice, computer club, Tai Chi, Weight Watchers, doctor's appointments, and the sports bar. We are so individualistic in today's world that it becomes difficult to define just what an American is. So, common sense is no longer common. Every individual is an expert for himself or herself. Today, we know more than football referees who call the games. Most of the yelling from the stands are from those who see the judgments differently. The doctor's appointment is not anything like it was years ago. Now we each know more than the person with seven years' education in medical school and twenty-five years of experience.

So, consider these two ideas together and reflect. Ponder sense or common sense as it intersects with moderation or extremism. More simply asked, "How can we know whether to follow moderation or extremism, given our lack of common sense, or perhaps any sense?" There are many who knee-jerk to every stimulus, rather than thoughtfully considering events, ideas, dialogue. We react in situations this way and that way with few standards for our behavior. Joseph Fletcher and others came up with the idea of "Situational Ethics," but I don't think they intended that we abandon all of our foundational learnings.

What good is the moderate lifestyle? Let's start with food. Is it better to starve and eat nothing or binge until our bodies hurt, or is it better to eat the necessary amount, the correct balance of good food groups and quantities thereof? Where is moderation between the extremes? Somewhere in between the extremes.

Should we adopt a motionless lifestyle? Only the drive-up window for us. No walking. Become the consummate couch potato? Flip that to the opposite extreme. Should we spend six hours in the gym every day of the week? Or should we pick somewhere in the moderate middle, being active, walking some each day, doing a little yoga and a reasonable workout?

The reflective reader may be thinking, "Hey, wait a minute. What about the cage fighter or the Olympian athlete? Don't they have to push their bodies to extremes?" There are always exceptions to moderation. The question is, "Does moderation make common sense?"

Let's introduce "socialism." It seems an easy segue. There are those who shout the word as if it were some sort of evil, devil-driven, abnormality, an enemy above all enemies. Not. It's simply a political ideology, a concept for how people can live and work and be together.

Throughout human history, every part of the world had slaves. There still are slaves. However, it is socialist thinking that has mostly led to the end of slavery in most places. There is only one question to the slave-owner: "As you desire to be free, don't your slaves want to be free also?" "No," is not an acceptable nor common answer. Common sense and socialism assert that all people desire to be free. It is a truth now written into our US Constitution. It is a worldwide accepted and common truth. We desire to be free. How can freedom and slavery co-exist?

It took until 1920, when the 19th amendment was passed, that women could vote. How long it took for a concept to rise to the top from centuries of suppression. Women want to vote as much as men. It's a common concept, common sense. It would be uncommon to suggest that they don't.

F.D.R. fought hard to achieve Social Security in 1935. It took another thirty years for Medicare. They were programs for the common good, because they made common sense. Shouldn't retirement income benefit all citizens, not exclusively the rich? Shouldn't health care be available to all citizens, not exclusively to the rich? Eisenhower had to lobby for an interstate highway system. If there is any reader of these thoughts who remembers crossing the country on secondary roads, you must believe the interstate highway system is a godsend. Why was it done? For the common good and because it made common sense. It was the driving force of socialism that achieved many of the benefits we all enjoy today.

In the 1930s, books were delivered by women to rural America as part of the public works post-recession recovery. Public libraries did exist in cities, but there were few in small towns. Wouldn't all want to read and learn? So, socialism, the common good, drove books into the hands of thousands and millions of those who would not otherwise have enjoyed the resource.

Taxes are a curious entity. I suppose if a world poll were taken, three quarters of the population would want to do away with taxes. People are always complaining that they have to pay taxes, that taxes are too high, that everything is being taxed, that there are fees and add-ons to everything. The short-sighted throw up their hands and shout out, "What good are taxes anyways?"

Few have sat down and listed the benefits of taxes. Wouldn't it be interesting if we just had dirt paths through the woods as we drove here and there. You can thank taxes for the paved, plowed, repaired roads outside your front door. In the good old days, folks threw their garbage and waste out the window. This led to the bubonic plague. Today, trash trucks and hard workers take your garbage away. We could make a long list, and it would be prudent to do so, as we together understand how taxes exist for the common good and make common sense. Yes, the concept of moderation enters in.

America is a socialist country but fears to admit it. Others proudly defend their form of government. In many Scandinavian countries, people receive all the education they want, all the child care they want, all the health care they want, all the retirement and disability income they need, and so on. They may pay 60% of their income for taxes for these common benefits. That leaves 40% of their income for housing, food, transportation, and entertainment. If a family earns $60,000 a year, they have $24,000 left for personal spending: $8000 for home, $4000 for car, $6000 for food, and $6000 for entertainment. Some Americans can spend $24,000 a year on their health care, and $200,000 for a four-year college education. An often-heard rebuttal is "Those are small countries; socialism wouldn't work in America." There is no basis for that statement, no supporting facts. Common sense. Common good. If the extreme wealth of the very top 1% of America were equally distributed to the common, every family would be supported to a much higher degree, and the wealthy would still live very well.

Scandinavians believe two things. They believe their country's greatest resource is its people. America believes its greatest resource is its wealth. Scandinavians believe that when their citizens don't have to worry about medical bills, education, child care, and a host of other needs, their minds and time can then be freed up to solve other problems which the nations face. Their infrastructure is years beyond America's. Their buildings are modern and eco-friendly. Their economy is stronger. They live longer and are healthier. It makes common sense to do for the common good, not out of resentment, but joy.

In the end, it's what makes sense to you. Extremism is an option. Moderation and common sense should be considered as well.

29

CONTROL

"**I WAS DRIVING** along, officer, and I just lost control of the car."

"How did that happen? Did gremlins take over?"

How does a person lose control of an automobile? Maybe a bump in the road jarred one's grasp on the steering wheel. Maybe an irate passenger stepped on the gas petal. Maybe a sparrow flew into the window and startled the driver. The point is, one lost control.

We lose control of many things. We lose control of our tempers and give way to anger. We lose control of our children when they rebel against our authority. We lose control of our possessions when we misplace them. Where are my car keys? We lose control of our health. We lose control of our sanity. We lose control of our business as it takes a downturn.

We don't like losing control. We don't give up control easily, and it is difficult living without control.

A question to consider is "Why is control so important to us?" We like control because with control, things happen the way we want them to happen. We want the world to be the way we want the world to be. At its base, control has to do with selfishness. We don't want "others" to rule our lives. I want me to control my life. The implication is "trust." I trust me, and I don't trust others as much.

Child-rearing is often a matter of child-controlling. Some parents raise children to think for themselves, make decisions for themselves, live for themselves. Other parents want a clone of themselves. They want their children to be just like they are, having the same values, thoughts, behavior. These are the parents that dole out approval of their children only when the children behave as they expect they should.

Of course, many a child rebels against this kind of control. A book was popular some years ago entitled *MAN THE MANIPULATOR, the inner journey from manipulation to actualization.* Most humans don't like being manipulated or controlled. They want self-determination. So dictators and tyrants are in constant struggle against those they seek to oversee.

Religious evangelicals want to control others. They think of it as conversion, rebirth, salvation. But as its basis, it's simply an effort to change others (who don't think like they do) into those who do think like they do. Proselytism is, at its heart, a terribly selfish endeavor. Why would somebody else think they have a better idea of how I should live my life? It is my life. I will choose to live it exactly as I want to live it, without your control – thank you very much.

Of course, there are some elements of society which must be controlled if society is to survive. Murderers, rapists, thieves will continue in their uncontrolled ways unless they are controlled. Humans have left a bloody river of attempted control.

The teens of the human species are the most idealistic. Their ideals seem to pull them ahead out of the stark realities in which they live. They dream of how things might be better and believe that better is possible. So, they attempt to control with demonstrations, marches, protests. Sometimes, they are able to push the machine of life a little to the left or right, but the degree of control always falls so short of their aspirations. Then youth become older. It's like the zeal is slowly leaking out of them.

When one reaches the mature years – what is that range? Forty to seventy? Fifty to one hundred? At some point, mature people wake up and think to themselves that they have control over very little, if anything. Instead of our earlier images of our strongly swimming against the raging current of life, we now consider the image of a leaf gently flowing down a stream, not ever able to turn right or left. Instead of being a person with control, we think of ourselves as being controlled, if not completely, then nearly. No young person can understand or believe this. Such is the way it is when one has one's whole life yet to be lived.

Some accept this impending reality. Some fight against it. "Do Not Go Gentle Into That Good Night," a poem by Dylan Thomas, urges us to control until our last breath. Yet it seems that just at that point when a person has accumulated a truckload of life's experiences that could result in some wisdom to share, nobody wants to listen. So much for trying to control even at the end.

30

SCARS

THE OPENING SONG from the play, MAN OF LA MANCHA, raises many questions about striving, sacrifice, ideals, struggle, purpose, destiny. This song refers to a man "torn and covered with scars." He must have been quite a sight to look at. What about myself, I think. Am I covered with scars? Surprisingly so. Here's a short list.

- Stepped on a nail in a board while playing in a barn
- Six-inch compound fracture of the right leg at seven years old
- Several related scars related to the leg break
- Repair of three hernias
- Four-inch scar from motorcycle accident
- Vasectomy
- Frostbite scar on wrist
- Cut to thumb requiring three stitches
- Severed arm tendons, four-inch wrist scar
- Cut a finger requiring three stitches
- Removal of pre cancer under right eye

- Two wens removed from scalp
- TWo cysts removed from shoulder
- ICD implant
- One cyst removed from back
- Six heart catheterizations
- Scalp wound from sailboat boom
- Exploded eye artery
- Perforated tympanic membrane
- Knee scars from bike falls

There are over thirty scars of various sizes, shapes, severity, and locations, not to mention dozens of injections and IV's over the years. There have been lots of stiches, lots of pain, lots of healing. Another discussion might be over why I accumulated so many scars. Was it genes or stupidity or simple accidents? I don't think many of my scars were of the Don Quixote de la Mancha ilk, that is, achieved for the sake of honor and valor. I don't remember getting any of my scars as I was reaching out for the unreachable star. I'm also fairly sure that the world is not better for any of MY scars.

The human body is an amazing instrument. What actually is it who assembles the troops and barks out the orders, "We've got another bleed here; bring out the clotting and scar tissue and get this closed before the man bleeds out?" How does the body know why, when, and how to scar? I'm sure it can be explained biologically, that this goes here and that goes there and presto change-o, there's a scar. But isn't it all sort of a wonder?

I heard a doctor once say that the body was, after all, nothing more than a sack of water. We know that we are mostly fluid, and the body scars to keep the fluids we need inside. When there's too much blood flowing to the outside, we're called dead. Time and again, scar tissues have come to the rescue to stop the bleeds.

Let's move on to emotional scars. They are invisible, of course, but we are covered with them. Our emotions have been attacked and bombed our entire lives. A great list might be compiled: love's heartbreak, rejections, failure, death of a family member, being fired from work, bullying, rape. Most times, we heal from these wounds. Sometimes, some people do not heal. They walk among us with open sores and emotionally bleed out slowly.

I'm writing now in the midst of the world's COVID-19 virus crisis. At this moment, we don't know how this coronavirus pandemic will end, how many people worldwide will become ill, and how many will die. This has resulted in a financial crisis with the DOW stock market dropping from 30,000 to 18,000 in just days. This is a deep wound which will result in a big scar. Some may remember the stock market crash of 1929 which led our country into the Great Depression. Many carried scars for years from that wound. Others literally jumped out skyscraper windows and bled out.

One might reflect upon why things are the way they are. Couldn't creation have been put together in a better way? Why is it that we become wounded so many times in life? Why is it that life is such a vulnerable commodity? Why couldn't we have been built with the armor plate of the tortoise or armadillo? Why? Why?

Or we could flip the coin over and marvel at the body's ability to heal and scar. We were given a wonderful defense mechanism, a built-in powerful army of soldiers who stand ready to respond. While scar tissue isn't quite as good as the first skin we were given, it serves a great purpose. When we're old and grey, parts of our bodies may not be as soft and pliable as a baby's, but what we have left will suit the purpose.

Hail to scarring. Hail. Hail. And thank you, wonderful body, for being an ally to me my entire life.

31

KEEP THE SIMPLE, SIMPLE SO YOU CAN HANDLE THE COMPLICATED

MY FATHER OWNED just one new car his entire life. He bought a brand-new 1961 Plymouth Valiant, a smaller sedan, blue in color. It had a three-on-the-floor stick shift with an engine so small the car strained going up hills.

But my father loved that car. It was his pride and joy. We were driving through town one day in the new Valiant, and this young teen was clowning around on his bike, zig-zagging here and there, standing on the seat, and generally taking up a lot of the road. Dad waited for his moment to pass when he thought it was safe, and just then the boy on the bike swerved in front of the car.

We collided. The boy went flying onto the berm. His bike went under the car, looking like spaghetti when it came out the back end. The boy, thankfully, was fine. Dad walked to the front of his Valiant to inspect the damage. There was a tiny scratch or two.

When everyone caught their breath, the boy blurted out in tears, "Look at my bike!" Dad responded, "Look at my car!" He loved that car.

One day the Valiant engine was coughing and sputtering. Then Dad started coughing and sputtering as well. "It could be bad gas. It might be the carburetor, maybe the points. We'll have to take it down to Johnny's and pay for a repair." The car limped the five-block drive to a local garage and Dad's favorite grease monkey. Dad was in a panic. "It's my car, Johnny. It's real sick."

Johnny looked under the hood for about three seconds, and said, "Start 'er up." The Valiant purred like a kitten.

Dad bolted out of the car with the face of incredulity. "What was it, Johnny?"

"Just a spark plug wire; it just came off."

Dad muttered the maxim which I still remember, "I guess I'll just look for the simple solution first, before making things more complicated than they need to be."

There is a corollary saying, "Don't make a mountain out of a molehill." People do this. In relationships, people often make conversations more complicated than they have to be. Of course, maybe that's the inadequacy of the English language. A friend of mine, a PhD in mathematics liked to say, "Word are an awfully poor way to communicate." I suppose numbers are more exact.

But people do read into what others say. They filter an uttered sentence through their own vast experience. They often hear something other than what the speaker thought he or she said.

In Biblical studies there are two paradoxical words. The first is exegeses, which means that one pulls out from a sentence to understand what it objectively states. The second is eisegesis, which means that one puts into a sentence to understand what it subjectively states. Exegeses attempts to understand simply what a sentence says. Eisegeses is the putting of myself into the sentence and understanding what it says by the complication of my interpretation. Eisegeses makes conversation more complicated because one is adding the complexity of two humans' understandings into one conversation. Exegeses is the attempt to remove the "I" from the sentence and understand the words for just what they say. In short, it is the difference between objectivity and subjectivity.

One of my old friends used to say, "We have lost the art of conversation." I believe that what he meant by that is that we do not communicate as effectively and clearly as we once did. I submit evidence No. 1 – faces buried in a cell phone, texting, tweeting, etc.

I submit with all the available communication technology available in our current age, which should have made communication clearer, it has simply made it more complicated. We misunderstand more than we ever did before.

Innuendo, speculation, second-guessing, suggesting, muddy the conversational waters. A husband speaks to his wife, and the conversation begins.

I like your new haircut.

What? You didn't like the way I looked before?

No, I was just saying that I noticed you've been to the beauty salon, and you look beautiful.

I wasn't beautiful before? I'm not sure I like this new cut. What do you think?

I told you, I think she did a nice job. You look beautiful as always.

Well, I couldn't be beautiful with the old hairstyle and beautiful with the new hairstyle also. You really thought I was ugly before, didn't you?

No, dear, no, I didn't say that. I just said I like your new hairdo.

How could you have put up with me over all those years and not tell me how ugly I looked?

Yes, the conversation may be funny. It's tragic as well. We avoid the easy fork in the road and choose the more complicated. We waste energy and time on issues that are easy. We should be storing up resources for the more complicated challenges.

I'll mention only two complicated challenges: government and aging. First, government. Everyone has an opinion. I know that's our right as free American citizens to express our ideas about everything. But there is a reason why professionals are call professional and experts called experts. They know more about their particular fields than we might know. Yet we yell at the referees on the playing field, shouting out, "That a bad ball; kill the ref." We think we know more than our doctors when we come in for a visit. We certainly think we know more than our elected officials at whatever level we're talking about.

I, for one, think the issues are terribly complicated. The citizenry wants more services with less taxes. How can that work? Society at large is screaming advice at those who are on the front lines, those who have first-hand and up-front experience with the issues at hand. We want to vote out all senators and congressmen who never do anything right. I suggest that the problems are complicated and the possible solutions are even more so. Why is it that poverty and ignorance have not been eliminated? Do we think that good, smart people have not been working on the issues? If the best of brains and moral people have not cracked the nut over hundreds of years trying in every culture around the world, what makes us think that we each know the answers? There are protests all around us. This is our right. But in the midst of our righteous indignation, in the middle of my self-assured correctness, can we not honor and admit that there are many perspectives to consider? I don't think I'll run for elected office. I give a tip of the hat to anybody who puts themselves into that boiling pot.

Aging. Young people have all the options of life. The process of aging is the gradual elimination of one choice after another. It's a sad note of reality, one that older folks have kept secret all these years. We don't want to upset those coming along.

Ultimately, we who are aging fast have only one thing to look forward to – death. As our bodies, minds, and spirits gradually deteriorate, as we lose this ability and that, we all see what is ahead.

- You're too weak to ride a bike.
- You must now take these three medications to keep your illness at bay
- You can't see to drive. Surrender your license.
- You can't take care of yourself anymore.
- We're going to have to remove that breast, finger, leg, etc.
- You're getting your meds mixed up.
- You could have surgery, but it may only buy a few months

Aging is the accumulation of losses. Much of it is guesswork as concerns what to do. If we choose this, we lose that. Or this choice might be slightly better than that choice. Or is it? Life is easy if you die young. If you age, life becomes more and more complicated. One would think it would not, but it does. Sorry for the bad news.

What's the suggestion, then? Keep things as simple as you can as long as you can. The longer you live, the more complicated life will be. I used to say to everyone I knew, "Be a kid as long as you can be a kid. You'll have your whole life to be a grown-up and work." Being a kid is simple. Being an adult is complicated. Being an older adult is the greatest of life's challenges.

32

GHOSTS ARE REAL

WHEN I WAS four years old, there were ghosts living in our attic. That's a fact. I knew for sure they were up there. I heard them. I could not go to sleep at night until a certain problem was addressed.

This was years before the movie people became ghostbusters. I had a live-in ghostbuster called Mum. She remedied this particular problem every night.

We got bath time out of the way. Got the teeth brushed. "Good night, Dad; good night, brother," I yelled to the downstairs. Then I got into those funny flannel jammies. Next, down on the knees for prayers.

"Are you ready, Gary? Shall we take care of those ghosts?" she said.

"For sure, Mum."

She always carried a paper bag upstairs during the nightly routine. We'd sneak up the attic steps with a flashlight. She'd point it here and there. "Do you see any?" she'd ask.

"There's one there." I pointed.

Mum would scurry over, grab him by the neck and push him into the paper bag. "Any more?"

"There's one; there's another one." And so it went for quite some time, until we were sure we had every last one of those ghosts stuffed into that bag.

Down the steps we'd go, but Mum's work wasn't done. A few had slipped into my bedroom, and we had to nab those nasty fellas, too. "There's one behind the dresser. There's another one under my bed." Only when I was satisfied that we had every last one of those scary ghosts, did we both work our way downstairs.

We went right through the living room, then the kitchen, then out the back door. Winter or summer, it didn't matter. Mum rolled that bag into a big ball and I watched her as she squished that bag into the trash can and pushed the lid on hard. "Well, I think we got 'em all," Mum would say.

As we'd walk through the living room, very relieved, Dad would ask, "Did you get every last one of those ghosts?"

I'd say, "Yep, Dad, Mum got every last one of them." Up the stairs we both went again.

Into my bed I went. Mum leaned over to give me a kiss, and I smiled. I rolled to my side and was asleep before she left the room. I slept like a bug in a rug. But I wouldn't have slept a wink, not ever, if it hadn't been for the queen of all ghostbusters, my Mum.

33

THE WEAK AND THE STRONG

HE'S MENTAL. THAT'S what he is. He's got a screw loose. He's pulling with one oar. He's playing with a deck of fifty-one cards. Something's not right with that chap, I'll tell you. He's simply broken, damaged goods. Nothing good will ever come from that fella. He's a retard, an imbecile. His whole family was looney, never quite right in the head. Yeah, I think maybe he's bipolar, manic-depressive, or maybe just clinically depressed. Can't do much about that. I heard he's seeing a psychiatrist, regularly. He can't even hold a job. Who would hire him? His head's not right. I hear sometimes they have to tie him down. Imagine that?

We're not very kind to those with mental health problems. The above are just a few of the nasty, biting comments that can be heard, often whispered about those with mental illness. There is stigma attached to it for some reason. People don't like to even admit, much less talk about, their mental health problems.

Not so physical problems. New hips, cancer, tummy tucks, breast enlargements, bowel resections, open heart surgery. Oh, God, I was puking my guts out, and stuff was coming out the other end like Old Faithful. We will sit at women's tea and talk about our blood, and fluids, and cartilage, and bones without ever a thought of embarrassment, but if we have a mental problem? Hush. Hush.

It's all rather odd that we have this double standard. Physical illness is like the Red Badge of Courage. Meanwhile mental illness is the plague from Satan. "Hey, look here. See that hose coming out of my stomach. That's my poop. It goes right into a little bag here and that's all there is to it. Did I show you my scar from my appendectomy? They had to open me up from here to there. Isn't that something?" We're proud of our physical problems but ashamed of our mental problems. I don't know why that is.

For the time being, I'll just leave spirit to the side. But there's that part of us too. Mind, body, spirit. We can be healthy or sick in any part of who we are. For now, let's just talk mind and body.

Is it because those with mental illness often look weird? Their eyes sort of go this way and that, and their hair is always messed up. I don't think they look more weird than the chap walking around with artificial legs and feet or tied to a colostomy bag. That's weird-looking. So, it can't be that.

Why is it that physical illness equates to strength, and mental illness equates to weakness? They don't smell any different. Why do we put down those with mental illness so much?

Certainly, there's this Darwin fight among the species thing going on. Yes, as biological creatures, wanting the first crack at the females for procreation, we worship at the throne of physical health, bodily health. Nothing like a couple of rams banging their horns together on a hillside. Human courtship is not much above this. But I don't think this helps us solve the riddle.

Mental illness? From whence does it come? How does one's mind or brain get sick and break down? The causes are as myriad as for physical illness. There is stress, loss, death, broken relationships, heartache. There is physical damage to the brain as well due to birth defects or injury. We're understanding that genetics plays a large role in the mental health or illness of mankind.

Tourrette's syndrome, attention-deficit disorder, schizophrenia, borderline personality disorders, anxiety, all may come from the genes. It begs the question—if one has no choice over the problems one might be given from birth, then why do we blame people for having these problems? It is as insane as the child on the playground taunting another, "My creation was better than your creation. Nah, nah." Why do we do this?

They are seen as weak. They are not strong like I am. Weak is not important. They are a burden. Better dead than taking up valuable air that the rest of us need. Hitler's attempt to exterminate Jews and those with mental illness is the result of such twisted thinking. It is sinister thinking of the concept of survival of the fittest.

Thankfully, we may be getting wiser as a world. Just a few years ago, cancer was thought to be contagious. People with cancer were shunned. Alcoholism was seen as a weakness and not an illness to be cured. Slowly, slowly, societies are growing up.

Homosexuals lived in the shadows for years. Their suicide rate still leads that of many other groups. Now, we are understanding that there are all kinds of sexualities. People are born the way they are. No amount of "brainwashing" will change them. They do not need healing. They need acceptance and understanding. Today, we are beginning to realize that there are a many expressions of sexuality. Love comes in many sizes and shapes.

However, it must be said that those who hurt children or abuse animals or engage in other destructive sexual behaviors are outside acceptance. There is a line that must be drawn.

Getting back to acquired problems. If one breaks a leg, one

goes to those who know how to set it, cast it, heal it. If one breaks an emotion, one goes to those who know how to heal it and make us better. There should be no stigma attached to either. We are all broken in one way or another. We have all needed mending and healing. No one is stronger or weaker than the other.

34

CEMETERY RISINGS

IT IS A summer's sullen Saturday. I am pulled awake by some force. Is it a noise? No. It is the soundless beckoning from the lonesome valley. I gather my supplies. I will need a pail, yard tools, a whisk broom, small shovel, rake, some rags. I pack the car and head out. I am pulled, not in my usual directions, but to a location afar. I am driving to a cemetery, but not just any cemetery. It is the cemetery in which my ancestors' remains are buried six feet deep.

As I enter through the gate, I observe other cars parked off the windy dirt roads, just onto the grass. Others are kneeling on the ground at various distances. They are on pilgrimage, as I am.

Most don't bother with this ritual anymore. They have other concerns. Or perhaps they are too afraid. But we who kneel in the fraternity are those who sense the bond of kindship, who are connected by strong feelings which we cannot fight off.

I push away overgrown grass and weeds and collect old leaves. There, finally, are the markers. My father and mother are side by side. Dad was the first to go, far too young at age forty-five. I witnessed as he sucked in his last gasp of air. He was a good father. He fished with me. My mother, next to him, achieved eighty-nine years before she passed. She lived more years without him than with him. Our mothers are unique in all the world. They are those who have loved us longer than any other, at their first awareness of life in their womb.

My father's parents are buried a short distance away. Grandmother loved a good belly laugh at a dirty joke. Grandpa lived to be one hundred and one. He had a gravelly voice and was missing a finger on his left hand.

As I clean and tidy, I become flooded by so many memories I would not otherwise bring to mind, were I not there. Through the tears and the smiles as I work, I remember so much about the earlier days with them.

As I drive home, I am emotionally worn. But I am glad I made the effort. I don't think so often of those earlier days, unless I make the journey. I must pilgrimage to those who were so dear to me, so they will become dear to me once more. They are those who made me what I am. I need to remember that I will never be alone. There are cemetery risings. The saints above hover very near.

35

CORRECTING EACH OTHER

FOLKS WHO DON'T seem to understand the Holy Bible very well seem to quote a verse that leads them into irresponsibility. They pull it out whenever they've done something bad. It's a defense of sorts. It's short, pithy: "Judge not, lest you be judged." It's a psychological defense mechanism, used to help protect the ego.

They might just as well say, "You who live in glass houses better not throw stones." They spout these sentences to deflect attention away from themselves and back onto others. They offer these quotes to end a conversation, and usually, shortly afterwards, walk away, feeling intact and still protected.

One of my very good friends had an overweight brother. Oh, Gawd, he was so much more than that. As an appointed lawyer, he drove around with a trunk full of teddy bears to give to the kids. You know the kids? The kids who were being jerked around this way and that by parents who never should have become parents, parents who did nothing but fight with each other until they ended up in divorce court. You know the kids, the wounded kids, the fought-over kids, the kids who would wonder whether their parents loved them for the rest of their lives. This "overweight lawyer" would give the kids Teddy bears. "At least they should know their Teddy loves them," he would say.

This person whose wife took a year to die in intensive care visited that wife almost every day. It was a two-hour drive there, and a two- hour drive home. This person who sat at her bedside and read to his wife and talked with his wife, stayed by her side until she died. Then, he visited her grave daily after that.

This person was brilliant, extremely well read, kind to others. He was a good friend, whom I remember well. And he was overweight.

When he died, far too young, a good friend of his wrote a tribute in the local newspaper because their interests overlapped, and they knew each other well. This writer began his written tribute mentioning about how his friend could down five pizzas in a single sitting. But he didn't use the word overweight. He used a three letter word that begins with the letter "F," and he used this word several times. He made several comments about his friend's weight but continued with a good tribute.

When the sister of the man who died picked up the newspaper to read it, she was hurt deeply. She cried. "He was so much more than his weight," she said, sobbing. She impetuously wrote a letter to this man to explain why he was out of line.

She heard nothing for fourteen years. Fourteen years! Then, they ran into each other one day, and the man began with, "You wrote me a letter a long time ago." My friends thought she was going to hear it hard. "Well, I was pretty upset at the time," she said.

> Oh no. You were right and I was wrong. I've never forgotten that letter. It changed my life. I teach a course on journalism and I include your letter and this incident in every class I have ever taught. I use your letter as an example of what not to do. I didn't think there was much wrong with it. I was trying to be truthful. But I forgot one thing. I didn't think how my tribute would affect those who loved him most. Ever since I received

your letter, I think before I write about how it will sound to those who love another the most. Thank you for setting me straight. You'll never know how much your letter means to me.

So much can be learned from this. There are many powerful lessons. But the focus here is judging. My friend loved her brother. There's another scripture verse, much more important than "Judge not, lest you be judged." It is "Speak the truth in love." She loved her brother enough to speak the truth in love. She consequently judged the actions of another person in this situation. She was right to have done so. At the time, who knows what the outcome might have been. But the recipient received his correction for what it was.

My friend's letter did not come in the form of anger. She simply explained that there might have been a better way to do what he did. He listened. He changed. He changed for the better.

There are many occasions when we should correct others. Why? So that there will be peace between us. So that the air will be cleansed. So that another can be helped back on the straight and narrow path to walk in a better way.

There are many occasions when we should receive correction. Do we protect ourselves too much so that another's loving counsel cannot get to us? None of us is perfect. If somebody has tried to show you a better way, and have told you the truth in love, then you are loved because you were corrected.

Open your minds and hearts. Be listening as somebody may be loving you enough to correct you.

I have been corrected so many, many times. I take note of the fact that I must be loved by many. I must be important enough to them that they would give the time, make the effort, bother themselves to share with me something that they think I need to hear. This is how we are made better, if we listen, if we respond by changing our thinking and our behavior.

36

THEM THAT SAYS MORE THAN OTHERS WANT TO HEAR

IN THE EARLY days of America, in the 1700s to maybe the 1850s, the gospel message came to the early settlers by way of the circuit rider. The circuit rider was a preacher on horseback who considered his calling to spread the good news far and wide. As small towns were established, among the buildings erected were often a schoolhouse (whether or not there was a schoolteacher in town) and a church (whether or not there was a preacher in town).

So, it came to pass that preachers would ride the circuit from this town to that. The circuit rider preacher might serve ten or twenty small towns with many miles in between each one. Part of the parishioners' hospitality was to have the preacher over for dinner and put him up for the night. After a while, communities began to know about when the preacher would show up to administer services. It might be on a Tuesday morning, or a Thursday afternoon, or every third Saturday in the evening. So, folks were used to gathering whenever the church bell rang and they knew the circuit preacher was in their town.

On a day long ago, a harsh winter's day, one old farmer wandered down to the church in his town to prepare for the preacher's coming. The farmer knew the preacher would be along that day about three or four o'clock in the afternoon. The old farmer went inside, lit several oil lamps, and lit a good fire in the wood stove which stood in the center aisle of the church. There he waited for the preacher to arrive.

The circuit rider preacher did arrive, and the old man went to the narthex to peal the bell and summon the faithful. He rang and rang the bell, but nobody showed. He rang some more. Nobody else came to the church.

The preacher said to the old farmer, "Well, what do you think?"

The old farmer thought a spell, then began to rub his chin with his thumb and index finger. Looking up, he finally said, "Well (and he stretched that well out to wheellll) I don't know about you, but I know about me. If I took a load of hay out to the barn to feed the cows, and only one cow showed up, I'd feed him."

The preacher thought to himself – well, that's the nod. This old farmer wants me to go ahead with the service. And that he did. The preacher went to the pulpit and stood behind it. Together, the two of them, sang a hymn. Then, they said a prayer. Then, they read a psalm. Then, they read the scripture reading for the day. Then, the preacher began to preach.

It was a text the reverend was very familiar with, so he had a lot to say. The more he preached, the more he thought about the faith of that old farmer, who like the cows, desired to be fed, not with oats and straw, but with the living gospel word. The preacher was on a roll. He preached for a half hour, then forty-five minutes. He looked down and saw the farmer attentively listening. He preached for an hour, and finally stopped after one and one-half hours. They sang another hymn, had another prayer, stood for a blessing. Then, the preacher walked to the front of the church to await the old farmer's leaving.

They shook hands at the front door of the church. The

preacher said to the old faithful farmer, "Well, what do you think?" The old farmer thought for a spell, then began to rub his chin with his thumb and index finger. Looking up, he finally said, "Well (and he stretched that well out to wheellll) I don't know about you, but I know about me. If I took a load of hay out to the barn to feed the cows, and only one cow showed up, I wouldn't give him the whole load!

37

TEMPUS FUGIT

WHY WOULD A person do it? Why would anybody quantify time? Wouldn't you just like to take that chap out behind the barn and wring his neck? What was he thinking, anyway? Why would we need to attach numbers to time? What is magic about twenty-four hours in each day? Why not ten or eighty-one? Sixty minutes in each hour? Why? Why are there 360 seconds in every hour and 8,640 seconds in every day? What difference does it make? I've always been partial to 10,000. Why if we had to quantify time, couldn't there be 10,000 seconds in every day? Who measured the length of a second, anyway? What if it were just a little bit shorter or longer? Would it make any difference at all? Who came up with the scheme? As I said, if I ever find the chap, I'm going to give him (or her, as the case may be) a good knock on the head.

Tick-tock, tick-tock, tick-tock. Is there a sound so quite annoying as a mantel clock? What's it doing up there, just ticking and tocking? What difference does it make if the big hand is on six and the little hand on nine? Who cares? Why should we care?

We have given ourselves over to this beast. If it's 7 a.m., we must awaken. By 8 a.m., we must eat. Why and why? If it's 9 a.m. we must go to work, and at twelve noon, eat again. Why and why? What happens if I want to get up at 10 a.m. and eat at 3 p.m., or whenever I feel like doing either one? We are prisoners of the clockwork, of the time keepers--watches and clocks. Why would we allow a little mechanical or digital box to so control our living?

In the old days, whenever that was, it was the sun which ruled our lives. In agrarian times, the sun and seasons determined the rhythm of life. This force, the sun, is so much greater than a clock. The sun might better determine our living. Instead, we give over to the clock which tells us when we are tired, hungry, sexual, or happy. Consider the quantification of time, and ask why? Could one get through life without this bondage? Perhaps, even now your time piece is dictating to you. "You have a dinner date in ten minutes. You'll have to mark the page in this book and come back to it later. The clock-God says you must obey and so you must." I, for one, am advocating a protest, perhaps an uprising, even a revolution. Freedom. Freedom. Break free from the bondage of the clock and live. Of course, the choice is yours. Count the minutes or count life.

We refer to these clock gadgets as "time keepers." There is no keeping time. Time cannot be kept. Time cannot be saved. Time happens. Time goes. Tempus fugit is the Latin for "time flies." But time cannot be kept. Time is a free spirit, doing what it wants. Time passes, but it is not kept.

Let's slide over to a slightly different perspective on time. Let's consider the concept of prisoners "doing time." It seems an innocent enough phrase, until one puts on the moccasins of a prisoner and imagines just what it might be like to do forty years to life. Inside the walls and barbed wire, the clock ticks ever so slowly. Our minutes become their hours. Our hours become their days. Our days become their months and years. Doing time takes an awful lot of time. Only those who have done it can possibly feel the oppression. Time becomes a cruel enemy, the harbinger of monotony, the handmaid of boredom, that which sucks life from the ones inside. Could we come close to understanding "doing time?" Perhaps, if we remember the experiences of waiting for news of a loved one's surgery. Or can we bring to mind the social isolation during a COVID-19 pandemic? Even these are just a glimpse of "doing hard time."

It is a hymn of lament that prisoners sing. "Time, like an ever- rolling stream, bears all its sons away. They fly forgotten as a dream, dies at the opening day." In prison, some choose to end time. They jump. They hang. They otherwise die to be over and done with time. Time has not been their friend. Doing time is the opposite of tempus fugit, time flies. Doing time is slow time, miserably slow time, time that goes on and on.

So, we have: (1) clock time, (2) fast time, and (3) slow time. The slave-master clock time tells us how we should feel. In fast time and slow time, we feel or sense time.

What about "enough time"? Do we have enough of that? There are those who teach time management, that is cramming stuff into what they think is available clock time. "We're all given the same 24 hours in every day." Is that a criticism of those who don't accomplish enough in that time period? These are the people who grocery shop at 4 a.m. to avoid the crowds and "manage time." These are the people who return phone calls at 4:45 p.m., knowing that the folks on the other end of the phone will not waste time talking about this and that but get straight to the point, as they want to get home for supper. These are the people who have daily planners, blocked out in fifteen-minute boxes. These are the people who know precisely how long the local train takes as compared to the express. These are the people who live with "deadlines," knowing exactly the moment when the briefing must be ready. How many, indeed, have died trying to keep deadlines. These are the people who will say, "There's never enough time in the day to get everything done that I need to get done." They enjoy slavery. Otherwise, why would they do it?

At the end of the day, the question is "Before what will we kneel?" Will we give yourselves over to the tyrant clock, like a drone or zombie, and thoughtlessly obey? Or will we receive time as gift, as grace, as joy? Maybe only then will we understand the passage of time.

38

THE DAY CRASH DANCED

I MET CRASH at college. He was and is quite a character. He's so talkative and outgoing. He's got more friends than most. He has a crazy laugh that comes out in a blast after a long inhale. It's maybe like a foghorn. His body moves back and forth as he deals with his laughter. Crash was my college roommate one year. We've been friends for more than half a century. He might be my BFF. I was there for him when his father died, then his mother, then his brother. He was there for me when my mother died. We've cried so much, as men. And we've laughed, well, like hyenas.

We're all different in our own ways. Crash is different because of his cerebral palsy. It was caused when he was born – insufficient oxygen to the brain. CP is sometimes referred to as spastic paralysis. This results in a variety of muscle weaknesses. Crash has a right arm and hand that is tucked up to his chest, almost like the wing of a bird. One leg is shorter than the other, and he walks with a pronounced side to side motion. He got his nickname, "Crash," because he is always falling down and crashing into things.

When Crash was a kid, he didn't let his disability slow him down at all. With braces on his legs, he played tackle football with the neighborhood kids. When he and I used to play ping-pong, he would often beat the dickens out of me.

When we were in college, in my ignorance, I once said to Crash, "What must it feel like to walk so oddly? It's just not normal the way you walk."

With gentleness he responded, "The way I walk is for me my normal; it's the only way I've ever walked." Lesson #1 in disability awareness.

Crash wanted to marry a "looker," a beautiful woman. Many a beautiful woman would not give Crash a second chance because of his CP. Yet, Cupid finds ways. After being in the dating game for years, he married a West Virginia beauty with personality and charm, a beer-drinking wonder with a spirited sense of humor. And she is blind. Together they were married and we all sang, "Amazing Grace." Yes, "We once were lost but now are found, were blind but now I see." Not a dry eye in the church. Their blind organist played all the music and never missed a note. They have one wonderful son and now a beautiful granddaughter.

Crash and his wife are a pair like few others. They stay together when they go out. She is his legs and he is her eyes. Together they go everywhere. When their son was born, in order to prevent him from developing the same eye problem as his mother, they had to insert and remove contact lenses daily. There the child would quietly lie on his back on the dining room table, while his mother felt for his eyes and with her fingers pulled back the lids. Crash would then take a little applicator and insert the contact into the eyes. It was a wonder to behold the teamwork.

Crash graduated from college and had a full working career, employed many years by the Office of Vocational Rehabilitation. His wife works too as a skilled seamstress. Over the years I have learned so much from this family.

As folks with uninjured bodies, as our bodies age, we become stiffer. We live with aches and pains. We may acquire other problems such as high blood pressure or heart disease.

However difficult aging is for most of us, for somebody with a disability, it's much, much worse. Crash's body gets tighter and tighter. He loses muscle strength in already damaged muscles. He mostly travels in a three-wheeled scooter now, but he still drives, teaches at a college, and climbs stairs every night for bed.

Recently we celebrated our 50th college reunion and a grand bunch of us returned. It was great seeing old classmates we hadn't seen in decades. Even if we were not close with some, we got caught up and laughed.

At the homecoming game, our team got crushed. Oh, well. Tours of the campus were wonderful. After all these years, there were still three of our professors who attended the events. The Saturday dinner was yummy. Then someone said, as the music started, "I want to dance; anyone want to dance with me?"

Now at a 50th college reunion, there were a lot of walkers and wheelchairs. Probably half in attendance couldn't walk, much less dance.

Well, that was floating around in my mind as I glanced over to see Crash, sitting in his chair and giving me a smile. The gang never said a word to each other, but I think we all had the same thought. We are never going to have a night like this again, our 50th college reunion dinner dance. Carpe diem. This is the only moment we will have like this again, ever. Then a pixie sprinkled magic dust over our evening.

So, at the invitation to dance, whoosh, a large group jumped to their feet and pirouetted over to the small dance floor. Now, add to the scene, the best dance music ever. Songs that would make even those with two left feet want to get up and shake it. There were more than a few of them that night. Fellas and gals who were terrible dancers were out there on the dance floor having the time of their lives. We were dancing. We were drinking and dancing. We were dancing and laughing. We were dancing, drinking, and laughing. It was a

Cinderella night, a magic night like I've never had before. I think we all felt the same way. We threw caution and possible embarrassment to the wind. We didn't care if we didn't come off like Fred Astaire and Ginger Rogers. We were just dancing to life.

It was mostly mass chaos. We were dancing, not so much with one other, but with everybody, sort of in a circle. I glanced over to see Crash, sitting in his scooter, off to the side. *This will not be*, I thought. I went over and said, "Put that thing in neutral," and I pushed him right into the center of the circle. A cheer went up. Crash started shaking it. He was movin'. He was groovin'. He was swayin' and croonin'. Everyone was taking a turn, moving in towards him and smacking down some moves. He never got out of the scooter. He didn't have to. Crash was dancing like he never danced before. The floor was hot.

Everyone on that dance floor was a lifelong friend of Crash. It was a moment of such beauty, acceptance, memory, power. We old people were tiring ourselves out, yet we danced on and on. We were all celebrating our college time together, that we were all still alive. Without the words ever being said, we all knew our lives had been a blessing. We were together again (probably for the last time). And we were celebrating the day that Crash danced.

CPSIA information can be obtained
at www.ICGtesting.com
Printed in the USA
LVHW051648131220
674080LV00043B/2543